THE
CONFIDENCE
PLAN

HOW TO BUILD A
STRONGER YOU

Tim Ursiny, PhD, CBC, RCC

SOURCEBOOKS, INC.®
NAPERVILLE, ILLINOIS

This publication is designed to provide accurate and authoritative information
in regard to the subject matter covered. It is sold with the understanding that the
publisher is not engaged in rendering legal, accounting, or other professional
service. If legal advice or other expert assistance is required, the services of a
competent professional person should be sought.—*From a Declaration of
Principles Jointly Adopted by a Committee of the American Bar Association and
a Committee of Publishers and Associations*

Published by Sourcebooks, Inc.
P.O. Box 4410, Naperville, Illinois   60567-4410
(630) 961-3900
Fax: (630) 961-2168
www.sourcebooks.com

Library of Congress Cataloging-in-Publication Data

Ursiny, Timothy E.
  The confidence plan : how to build a stronger you. / Tim Ursiny.
     p. cm.
  Includes bibliographical references.
  ISBN 1-4022-0349-7 (alk. paper)
  1. Self-confidence. I. Title.

BF575.S39U77 2005
158.1--dc22

2005004109

Printed and bound in the United States of America
VP   10   9   8   7   6   5   4   3

For Jacki, Samantha, and Kyle, who have been through so much at an early age. Use your adversity to strengthen your confidence and your abilities to help others in need. Always remember to rely on God for your path.

For their mother and my sister, Christi. I still miss you.

CONTENTS

ACKNOWLEDGMENTS

Having talked with many authors this year I have come to realize more than ever how blessed I am to be working with Sourcebooks. Todd Stocke is an editor's editor and his input has been critical to the flow and purpose of this book. Thanks to his team, especially Samantha Raue, for their fine work in fixing those copy errors that were just invisible to me. My publicist, Angie Cimarolli, and the rest of the publicity team are a pleasure to work with and show great enthusiasm and devotion to getting the word out on *The Confidence Plan*. I feel that Norma Fioretti and her design team created a cover that really captures the feel of this book and I deeply appreciate their commitment to excellence. I also can't say enough about Dominique Raccah, my publisher and guide in this adventure. Her direction and heart are in this book in many ways. She has been a great mentor on this journey.

I am very thankful to my family for putting up with my crazy schedule and still loving me when I get too wrapped up in my projects. Zachary, Colton, and Vance are three sons of which any father would be proud. I love them with all my heart and hope that they live confident and caring lives. My wife Marla continues to be the glue that holds everything together. Without her support there is no way this book would have gotten done. She is simply incredible.

Much appreciation goes out to friends and colleagues who read this book and gave me their feedback. Especially helpful were Mark Anderson, Pat Woelfel, Barry Foster, Bruce Clinton, Sue Gage, Carole Smith, Carole Cowperthwaite and Barb Kay. Thanks for "speaking the truth in love" about your reaction to the stories and content.

I thank my mother, Frances Knight. She always believed that her shy and nerdy son should be dating the top cheerleader in high school. It makes a world of difference in your life to always have someone who believes in you. Special thanks goes to my stepfather Andy Knight who gave me my first "real" job and taught me business principles that I use to this day. I also thank my siblings, Kenneth Paul Ursiny and Jamie Ursiny, for their love and support. And while they have passed away, I do thank my father Kenneth Ursiny and my sister Christi for the same reasons. Each of my family members supported me in feeling good about myself even during the years that the world tried to tear my confidence down.

I thank all of my clients who allow me to walk down difficult paths with them. I continue to learn so much from you as we work together.

Finally, I thank God. I thank Him for the blessings, I thank Him for the lessons, and I thank Him for the grace.

INTRODUCTION:

A UNIQUE APPROACH TO CONFIDENCE

Our doubts are traitors, and make us lose the
good we oft might win, by fearing to attempt.

—William Shakespeare

What is Different About This Confidence Book?

There has been a revolution in psychology to move away from exclusively studying what creates dysfunction to looking at what makes people successful and happy. From Seligman's *Learned Optimism* to Marcus Buckingham and Donald Clifton's *Now Discover Your Strengths*, we are looking at people in a much more positive and proactive way. Despite this progress, many self-confidence books still tend to exclusively focus on those with low self-esteem.

In addition, most confidence books focus on a single method for building your confidence. The most common approach is to work on changing your self-talk and belief systems. While I am a firm believer in these mental strategies (and I cover them in section two), I believe that for most people they are just one piece of the confidence puzzle. My experience as a coach and psychologist working with thousands of successful people suggests that a single approach to building self-confidence is not usually effective for long-term confidence transformation. Instead, to truly upgrade our confidence we need to focus on a more holistic approach. We will do this by exploring the five different confidence-building methods of:

- Mental strategies
- Emotional strategies
- Behavioral strategies
- Relational strategies
- Spiritual/life purpose strategies

Together these form the five paths to confidence. Focusing on only one of these paths to confidence is like going to the gym and only exercising your biceps. You may get great biceps, but your body as a whole is not all that it could be. Or it is like trying to make a business successful by just focusing on its technology and ignoring marketing, people development, and business planning. No business can be successful if you just focus on one aspect. A multifaceted approach will beat a single faceted approach every time. This is especially true when it comes to developing ourselves as top performers and confident individuals. This book directly addresses all five of these paths to confidence in a systematic way in order to develop truly transformational self-confidence and breakthrough performance.

Many confidence books focus exclusively on personal lives. While this book can be used extremely effectively for your personal life, it is also built for people who want to increase their business success and people who want to help others grow their confidence. So whether you are an executive, a salesperson, a laborer, a mother, a husband, etc., this book can aid you.

Assumptions About You, the Reader

I know that assumptions can get you into trouble, but I am still going to start this book with a few assumptions. I am assuming that:

- You are a capable person who wants to grow more confident and/or help someone else become more confident
- You understand that confidence is a critical factor in achieving success
- You want a book based on solid psychological theory and research
- You want practical exercises to bring out your best level of confidence
- Since your time is limited, you want bite-size nuggets to digest and utilize each day
- You want actions that you can implement immediately
- You are open-minded and will consider several different paths to growing your confidence

If my assumptions are correct then this is the right confidence book for you.

How This Book is Structured

This book is laid out to provide you with maximum flexibility in how you read and use it. You can either choose to work this book at your own pace or you can approach this as a six-week program. I have divided each section to represent a week with seven days of readings or exercises around that week's topic. Therefore, chapter 1.3 would be the equivalent of week one, day three; chapter 5.2 would represent week five, day two. If you choose to follow this format, all you will need is an average investment of about twenty to thirty minutes a day for this structured path. Some chapters are a little longer and some may only take you ten minutes, but on an average time investment of twenty to thirty minutes a day for six weeks, you can and will upgrade your confidence to the next level. This may sound like work, but as coaching great Vince Lombardi said, "the dictionary is the only place that success comes before work." The six-week program with seven daily readings is further divided as follows:

The first chapter of each section/week is designed to get you ready for that particular approach to growing your confidence. These chapters contain humorous or introspective general examples from life and a preview of what is coming in that section. Chapters 2–6 in each section or week start with a quote and then are divided into:

THE RESEARCH:

Summarizes research on a psychological principle or type of statistic related to confidence (minus all of the psychobabble). I also include references for these studies at the end of each research section for those who would like to explore the original sources.

THE APPLICATION:

Explains how the principles discussed relate to our lives and confidence and expands on the ideas presented to make the application practical and meaningful.

THE ASSIGNMENT:

Contains questions and activities to coach you to your next stage of confidence. Exercises can be "solo" to do on your own or interactive to do with someone else. Additional assignments are also included in the back of the book for you overachievers out there!

In the final chapter of each section we explore a practical case study taken from individuals I have coached in the workplace (although the principles can be applied to the home also). All examples protect the identity of the client by combining client stories or changing identifiable details, but keep the integrity of the process intact. Each section ends with a challenge to you the reader to pick the techniques from that section that "speak" to you the most and apply them to your life. Within this format, you can spend about twenty to thirty minutes a day with the book and experience a huge payoff for that investment of time. Your experience will be even greater if you invite a friend or accountability partner to walk through the book with you.

Remember, if you always struggle with confidence then this book can help you. If you sometimes struggle with confidence then this book can help you. And if you think you never struggle with confidence, then this book can help you find those wonderful opportunities to struggle some so that you can go to the next level!

SECTION 1

GETTING STARTED

GET READY TO DEVELOP BREAKTHROUGH CONFIDENCE

It Makes You Wonder

"Oh, you're a guy—you'll do fine" were words that she would later regret. You see, I was soon to be married and had to get a steady job to support myself through school. I had worked throughout college at various jobs, including the position of "maintenance engineer" (i.e., janitor). So when I answered the job ad at a retirement village seeking a maintenance engineer, I was expecting a janitorial position. The woman who hired me listed duties that included landscaping, painting, and repairing broken toilets and faucets. I let her know that I had zero experience in these activities, but could clean the heck out of any toilet in the building. That is when she assured me that my gender would fix all of my inadequacies.

Over the next few weeks, I tried my best (inadvertently) to get fired. I was told to pull weeds from the perimeter. Unfortunately, I could not tell the difference between weeds and newly planted flowers. My boss was not amused. Then I was asked to fix a leaky bathtub. I don't even remember the cost of the water damage I caused. And about the damaged toilets…well some memories are better left repressed.

The final blow came when I returned from my honeymoon. I felt guilty leaving for a week so soon after being hired so I agreed to come in and work on Labor Day when no one else was around. I was wandering through the dark maintenance area when something slapped into my head. It was gooey and sticky and would not come out. Finding a light I discovered that flypaper had been put all over the maintenance room (minus the one strip that was in my hair). For the life of me I could not get this sticky substance out of my hair. Finally, with the help of industrial strength floor cleaner and lots of water, I removed the gooey substance.

As I congratulated myself on my ingenuity I turned and ran into another strip of flypaper. After another fifteen minutes of scrubbing, I managed to pull off the paper along with a good wad of hair. As I adroitly shifted through the maintenance area I was careful to avoid the remaining strips of pain…for a while. Yes, unbelievably while I was looking through the list of tasks my boss left me, another sticky strip reached and grabbed me (I swear those things were alive)!

Enough was enough. I washed my hair, wrote a note to my boss explaining that I had to leave and promised to tell her why the next day. Then I went home and told my wife, who I'm sure had doubts about me being able to pull my end of our financial burden (can you blame her?).

The next day I went into work and found my boss. She was talking with one of the residents and even from a distance, clearly looked unhappy. Upon seeing me, she started yelling across the room. "How could you leave me in the lurch like that?" she screamed. "Don't you know the meaning of responsibility?" As I tried to explain what happened, she shushed me and said that she had no interest in any of my excuses. I tried several times to clarify with her what happened, but she would not hear any of it. Not surprisingly, that was my last day on the job and I think we were both better off for it.

The Lesson

You have to be prepared for the job! Despite my boss's belief that my gender would fix my lack of experience, I obviously wasn't prepared for success as a maintenance man. Preparation—or the lack thereof—can determine the difference between doing well and doing poorly. Those who prepare well tend to do well. So before we dive into building your confidence to the next level, let's take a little time to prepare you for this transformation. Let's start by looking at the purpose of growing your confidence.

Why Bother with Growing Your Confidence?

We all intuitively know that confidence is important. Most of us know that if you always struggle with confidence then something is wrong. Either you are suffering from low self-esteem or you are working or living in the wrong place. It just doesn't match. However, did you know that if you never struggle with confidence, then something is also wrong? If you never struggle with confidence, you obviously are not stretching yourself far enough. You are not pressing to the edge of your abilities. In other words, the only way to never struggle with confidence is to play it safe. Play it known. Play it in a way that you achieve stability, but lose opportunity.

Businesses should care about the confidence of their workers. It is obvious when viewing a sporting event that the player or team that can tap into a higher level of confidence can dominate and turn the game around. Conversely, a player or team that receives a blow to their confidence can spiral down into an embarrassing defeat. The same is true for a corporation. A corporation with truly confident workers creates and takes appropriate risks. Corporations filled with lower-confidence individuals have an environment where people tend to play it safe, cover their behinds, and miss opportunity. This is especially true in times of transition. Fear is triggered by ambiguity and unless the corporation attends to the confidence of the workers, paralysis will occur.

Also, confidence plays a huge role in sales. People in sales have to be incredibly tenacious and persistent. An average level of confidence is a guarantee of mediocrity for the salesperson. People in sales need unusually powerful confidence to succeed and be happy.

In addition, corporations should care if their managers know how to inspire confidence in others. I have worked with countless top performers who have struggled greatly with helping people they manage also become top performers. Why? Well, many of these top performers do what they do naturally. If someone is struggling beneath them they often do not have complex strategies for helping because they have always just "done it." They often don't understand why others don't just do it too! Corporations would do well in investing in their managers' abilities to build confident employees.

Even in personal relationships confidence plays an important role. The higher your confidence, the more you can allow mistakes and imperfections in your significant other. Confident people can communicate more patiently and do not panic when a friend or loved one has a different opinion. On the other hand, lower confidence can be devastating. If you have ever been in a relationship with someone with low confidence then you know that feeling of having to "walk on eggshells" and watch every word so you don't trigger the person's insecurities or fears. "You don't respect me," might be the criticism, when the bigger truth is that the person does not respect him or herself.

Still not convinced that building your confidence is crucial? Just take the research on optimistic vs. pessimistic people. Famous researcher and author Martin Seligman defines these terms as follows:

- Pessimistic people believe that bad events will last a long time; optimistic people see these as temporary challenges
- Pessimistic people believe that negative events will undermine everything they do; optimistic people believe they can overcome them
- Pessimistic people believe it is their fault when they fail; optimistic people believe that defeat is due to other circumstances and remain determined to succeed

Who do you think does better in life? The research shows that there is no comparison. The optimistic or confident person succeeds over the pessimistic or low confidence individual in sports, business, relationships, and even in physical health and happiness.

However, as I mentioned, this book is not just for pessimistic people with low confidence. My goal is to help you become the most confident and optimistic person that you can be. While there is a lot of research concerning low confidence (and we will touch on some of that in this book), we don't want to miss the extensive research that has been done on normal levels of challenge and what makes people happy. So I am not going to take an abnormal approach in this book (i.e., assuming that you have deep issues with confidence and desperately need this book to survive), but rather I am going to assume that you are a capable and talented human being who wants to grow.

The Preview

The next six chapters are all about getting prepared for the confidence building methods that will follow. I want to make sure that we are on the same page concerning confidence. As I mentioned previously, one format is to work one chapter per day (for about twenty to thirty minutes a day on average). However, you may also just follow the book at your own pace. In the following six chapters we will:

- Dispel some myths concerning confidence and show why improving your level of confidence is crucial despite the level with which you begin
- Look at personal comfort zones and how changing your comfort zone setting takes discomfort and a challenge to your confidence
- Examine how failing can actually grow your confidence (if you do it right)

- Explore what drains our confidence
- Look at the core approach taken with this book of addressing five paths to confidence (mental, emotional, behavioral, relational, and spiritual) and clarify how each of these plays a slightly different role in your self-perception
- Determine your drive and motivation to upgrading your confidence

All right! We are going to start with the section where you pump yourself up to completely committing to doing this book for the following five weeks (or at your own pace). We will look at your confidence drive, build your motivation, and help eliminate anything that may block your success.

So let's get started. I will "see" you in chapter 1.2.

OPTIMISM IS NOT JUST FOR THOSE WITH LOW SELF-ESTEEM

Be humble, for the worst thing in the world is of the same stuff as you; be confident, for the stars are of the same stuff as you.

—Nicholai Velimirovic

THE RESEARCH: What Predicts Our Success

Do you remember the childhood self-esteem classic *The Little Engine That Could*? In this story there was a little train engine that was trying to get up the hill. The engine's success came with the mantra, "I think I can; I think I can." Well, that story is built on well-documented psychological theory. Initially, many psychological learning theories viewed people as controlled by external events (things that happened to them). However, in the mid-1980s Albert Bandura introduced a different point of view. He emphasized how we can be proactive and how our viewpoints or deeply held beliefs about ourselves can impact our lives. He called these beliefs about our abilities "self-efficacy." Research has shown that our expectation of success with a specific task is an incredible predictor of our success with that particular undertaking. In other words, just like the optimistic little engine taught us, it is good to "think you can."

Subsequent research has shown that self-efficacy is a powerful predictor for many behaviors related to stress and impacts multiple areas of our lives. Researchers building on Bandura's work have demonstrated how those with higher self-efficacy:

- Have greater tenacity when facing obstacles
- Maintained greater effort on tasks
- Have lower stress levels and greater serenity when dealing with challenges
- Expect more successful outcomes
- View difficult tasks as challenges to be mastered
- Have a greater sense of well-being and accomplishment
- Have faster recovery times after failure

Given these findings, you would think that all of us would be incredibly motivated to increase our self-efficacy to the highest point possible.

References: Piper, Hauman & Hauman, 1978; Bandura, 2001; Pajares & Schunk, 2001

THE APPLICATION

First we need to distinguish between self-efficacy, self-esteem, and self-concept. While there are many different opinions about the correct definitions of these terms, I view these differences as the following:

- **Self-concept:** Relates to the question of "who am I?" and involves assumptions that I have about myself.
- **Self-esteem:** The process of evaluating my character and performance against standards set by others or myself. In other words, taking my self-concept and judging myself as worthy or unworthy.
- **Self-efficacy:** How I feel about my ability to perform in a certain activity or situation such as my belief in my ability to play tennis well.

This brings us to the term that I will be using for the majority of this book, self-confidence. I see self-confidence as your overall belief in your abilities and talents. It is an optimism that prepares you to work through any challenge or roadblock. Thus, as I am using it, this term covers self-concept, self-esteem, and self-efficacy in combination to represent your overall view of yourself, your worth and your ability to get results. *The WorldNet Dictionary* defines self-confidence as "freedom from doubt, belief in yourself and your abilities." It also provides the synonyms of assurance, sureness, and authority. Therefore, it makes sense that anything that impacts your self-confidence would also impact your self-esteem, self-concept, and self-efficacy (and anything that impacted each of these would impact your self-confidence). The confident person is optimistic and believes greatly in her overall ability to reach her goals. However, let's not get too caught up in the semantics, but rather focus on building each one of these.

Characteristics of Truly Confident People

When I started doing my radio tour for my last book, *The Coward's Guide to Conflict*, I was pretty impressed with myself. I mean, here I was going on the radio to speak wisely about conflict and relationships. Certainly, I must be someone of significant importance! In one of my first interviews, I had a healthy dose of reality. I called up the radio station at our assigned time and I got introduced to my New York host. Over the phone she sounded like the "coffee talk" lady from old *Saturday Night Live* episodes. Within the first minute of the interview she was asking for my sage advice concerning conflict. Oh, not for her, mind you, but for her dog, Bobo, who had come into the studio with her that day. So here I was, Dr. Tim Ursiny, expert on dogs in conflict. Actually, she was a wonderful host and the interview turned out to be a lot of fun, but it thankfully reminded me to stay grounded.

One myth about confidence is that it is the opposite of humility. People sometimes even equate confidence with arrogance. I believe that this is a mistake. Rather than being the opposite of confidence, I believe that humility is an entirely separate issue. Looking at the following chart you can see how different combinations of self-assurance and humility might work together.

For example, someone with low self-assurance and low humility is often the braggart who is constantly trying to build himself up by praising himself. In truth he cares way too much about what others think of him and is covering up his low confidence. He is

	Low Self-assurance	High Self-assurance
Low Humility	Impostor	Arrogant
High Humility	Insecure	True confidence

an impostor. In contrast, someone with high self-assurance and low humility doesn't care at all what people think of her! She is arrogant and self-centered. Someone who has low self-assurance and high humility is likely insecure and self-doubting. He doesn't believe in himself and doesn't embrace his gifts. Finally, we have the person with high self-assurance and high humility. In my mind, this quadrant represents the truly confident person. She can fully embrace and celebrate her strengths and talents, and yet never forgets her humanity. She can admit mistakes and failings and yet never feel like a failure. She lives in gratitude for the gifts she has been given and never fails to see the giftedness in others. These elements make up true and lasting confidence.

So you might be thinking, "Well Tim, in all humility, I feel pretty good about my level of confidence." If that is the case, then great! However, you can still benefit from growing your confidence. Confidence can be built to the next level from any starting point. No matter what your level of confidence, you will benefit from improving it, especially if you keep your humility intact or grow it at the same time. Just think what you could accomplish if you were truly free from doubting yourself! On the surface we can look like a pretty confident culture. However, the number of unnecessary conflicts, hidden secrets, and work performance issues suggest that we could still grow quite a bit.

In her book, *Confidence: How Winning Streaks & Losing Streaks Begin & End*, Rosabeth Moss Kanter makes a great case for the power of confidence. She cites example after example of how confidence has impacted the winning and/or losing streaks of companies like Gillette and Continental Airlines, or teams such as the Chicago Cubs and the University of Connecticut women's basketball team, or individuals such as Nelson Mandela. Did other companies, teams, and individuals lack confidence or did these other people simply have the competitive edge of an incredible level of confidence?

In any situation where two people are competing with relatively similar skills, the more confident person will always succeed at a greater level. I don't care if we are talking about business success, parenting, competitive sports or even charity work, confidence can give you that extra edge to handle challenges effectively and meet the goals you want. Do you have that competitive edge? Do you model excellent confidence to your boss, peers, or even to your children? Even if you are completely satisfied with your level of confidence, do you know how to raise the confidence of those around you? If you are a business owner, a manager, a concerned family member, friend, or parent, you can have a great impact on the confidence of those around you using the principles we will be covering in this book. As the chapter title says, you do not need to have low self-esteem to want to know how to build, nurture, and protect optimism and confidence. Freedom from doubt and being able to help others free themselves also is an incredible gift to have and to give.

THE ASSIGNMENT

Fill out the following confidence wheel. Within each of the following eight areas, circle the number that best represents your overall level of self-confidence in that particular area.

Now, connect the dots. The rounder the wheel, the more balanced your confidence. Use this insight to help you work through the rest of this book and focus on those areas of confidence in which you would like to grow!

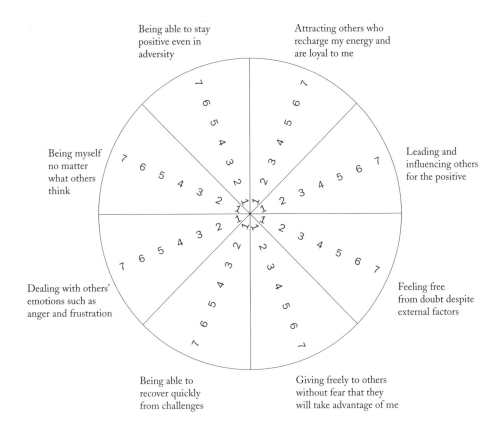

1.3

NEW CHALLENGES REQUIRE A NEW LEVEL OF CONFIDENCE

All of us have wonders hidden in our breasts, only needing circumstances to evoke them.

—Charles Dickens

THE RESEARCH: DRIVE AND BALANCE

Homeostasis is a scientific term to describe the fact that many things strive for balance. Just think of it as a set thermostat. When the room gets too cold, the heat turns on to move the temperature to the degree set on the thermostat. Once the room reaches the desired temperature, the heat turns off. If for some reason the room gets too hot, then the air conditioning kicks in to cool down the room. The purpose of the thermostat is to regulate the temperature and keep it at the level that you want.

Drive reduction theory suggests that when our homeostasis is thrown off, a drive is created inside of us that moves us to take some action that will restore balance and eliminate the tension that is created by the imbalance. In everyday language people talk about this as staying in their "comfort zones."

Reference: Hull, 1943

THE APPLICATION

We each have an internal thermostat when it comes to success. We have a level beneath which we will not let our success or failures fall (in AA they call this hitting bottom and this point is different for different people). I think that most of us know this intuitively. At some point we say enough is enough and we get working to make things better. But the range of difference between people is incredible. One person can't stand not getting promoted each year while another can stay on welfare and not seem to be bothered by it. This difference can be explained by many factors including models we had growing up, life experiences, and our perception of the world and ourselves. Again, most people realize that we have a point beneath which we will not allow ourselves to fall. What seems to be less well known is that most people also have a point of success that they will not let themselves rise above!

How many people have been plodding along the road to success only to shoot themselves in the foot before reaching all that they can be? There just seems to be something inside that subconsciously says, "Nope, this is as successful as I'm going to allow you to be." In fact, in human development fields like therapy and coaching it is a common occurrence that people have a relapse often because they were making such great progress. An example of this was a woman named Melanie who contacted my office for some one-on-one coaching. Melanie had everything going for her. She was the top female executive in her firm, she was well respected by her boss and her peers, she had a happy home life and she had far surpassed every financial goal that she had ever set for herself. Basically, she had everything going for her. However, despite her success, she was feeling confused and uncomfortable. Paradoxically, she had nothing in her life to feel badly about and therefore she was even more confused about what she was experiencing.

Through some short-term coaching Melanie realized that she was uncomfortable with how easily her success had come to her. She had grown up poor and only able to get through college on grants and working part-time. She knew that she was driven, but never thought she would have achieved what she had accomplished in such a short time. It just felt "weird" and wrong to her. She was in uncharted waters and did not have a map to navigate her way. Eventually, Melanie was able to overcome these feelings by resetting her expectations of what she was capable of and raising the temperature on her thermostat. She learned to play simple mind games like interpreting the uncomfortable feelings as a "good" sign that she was breaking through a false concept of herself that use to feel comfortable. She started using the analogy of needing to get rid of an old pair of jeans that served her well for years, but were now worn down and needed to be replaced with new jeans. In time, she felt entirely at home with her success.

Why are we so drawn to an inferior concept of ourselves and so thrown off by going beyond our own expectations? We explain this phenomenon the same way that we account for why a child of an alcoholic is often attracted to an alcoholic as a mate. We are drawn toward the known. We are comfortable with the known. And we are frightened by the ambiguity of the unknown. A child of an alcoholic knows what it is like to live with an alcoholic. She may not know what it is like to live with someone who is responsible, caring and centered on her feelings. While these things may sound good to her, they have not been experienced and therefore, when she does experience these good qualities, it may feel wrong, uncomfortable, and unknown.

Taking all of this together we see that our internal success thermostat is subconsciously set with a high point and a low point. The high point may be, "I will never allow myself to be more successful than my father" and the low point might be, "I will never make less than (X amount of money) per year." These points differ greatly for each of us.

So how this applies to our conversation is that you have to be aware of your high point. What is the point of success that you may subconsciously sabotage if you are not insightful and disciplined? The action steps presented in the next section can help you determine and prevent this.

THE ASSIGNMENT

At what point is your internal thermostat set? It is good to know the lowest level of failure that you will allow, as well as knowing your current goals. However, perhaps the most important thing is to understand at what level of success you will start to feel awkward. What is your beyond goal (this is a goal barely within the bounds of reality that makes you uncomfortable to really pursue)? What goal have you considered that makes you uncomfortable? Think specifically about a goal that makes you uncomfortable because of the chance for failure or the amount of work that it would take you to get there.

Something that I want to achieve, but I am unsure of, is:

_____

_____

As you work through the rest of this book, consider going after this "beyond goal." Make sure that your internal thermostat is set to the temperature that you want (not just the one that makes you comfortable).

1.4

HOW BEING KNOCKED DOWN CAN ACTUALLY GROW YOUR CONFIDENCE (IF YOU DO IT RIGHT)

Not only so, but we also rejoice in our sufferings, because we know that suffering produces perseverance; perseverance, character; and character, hope.

—Christian Bible, New International Version, Romans 5: 3-4

THE RESEARCH: Resilience and Secrets of Success

Resilience is a quality that allows us to pick ourselves back up after experiencing hardships or trauma. It is like the boxer who is knocked down, but not knocked out. He picks himself back up off the mat and continues the fight, many times turning the momentary defeat into victory. Researchers have studied resilience to determine what factors were most closely related to children developing this important characteristic. They discovered that the following factors were highly correlated with resiliency:

- Intelligence
- Talent
- High self-worth
- An easygoing disposition
- Faith

These characteristics helped individuals stay resilient through all sorts of traumatic situations including disasters, war, violence and poverty.

Along with resilience it is also useful to look at research concerning people who have been successful. In his book *The 100 Simple Secrets of Successful People*, David Niven, PhD, examined research on the characteristics of successful individuals. Several studies that he refers to describe the role that past experiences have in our success. These include findings that:

- Persistent people spend twice as much time thinking about past accomplishments and their ability of accomplishing a future task than less persistent people (Sparrow, 1998)
- When people think about things that they regret in life, eight out of ten are sorry about actions that they did not take as opposed to actions they did take (Ricaurte, 1999)
- According to Robeson, 1998, individuals who return to college a second time after failing at their first attempt believe that the

crucial factor to success the second time around is due to greater knowledge of: their selves; their capabilities; and their commitment.

References: Marsten & Coatsworth, 1998; Niven, 2002.

THE APPLICATION

Some people start off their lives with a decent level of confidence only to have their optimism erode as life events beat them up. I have worked with people in their forties and fifties that many people would have perceived as highly confident individuals. However, these clients had gotten knocked down in some way. Some of them experienced failure for the first time in their life and didn't know how to handle it. Others had experienced a series of unfortunate events that slowly decreased their confidence to make good decisions or find success. Their previous level of optimistic living seemed nowhere to be found.

These individuals were allowing life to steal their confidence. However, some people get knocked down initially only to get back stronger on the next time around. Abraham Lincoln is the classic example of this. He failed as a farmer. He failed as a businessman. He had a nervous breakdown. He was defeated for State Legislature, Speaker, U.S. Senate (twice), and for a Vice President nomination. And these are just a few of his "failures." So how did this man who failed so much become one of the greatest and best-remembered presidents in our country? He never stopped. He never gave up. He believed in something in himself and kept going. His tenacity and perseverance are a shining example of what you can accomplish if you believe in yourself enough to get up, brush off failure, and try again.

Or take the less historical example of comedian Jerry Seinfeld of the award winning television series *Seinfeld*. Initially, the network turned down his pilot. They said it tested poorly and audiences just did not get it. Then when they finally ordered the show they only ordered four episodes (perhaps the lowest order in history for a television show). The network fought to change the tone and style of the show on many occasions and yet Jerry Seinfeld and company held strong to their belief in what the show should be. Eventually, their confidence and ability to handle momentary setbacks led to incredible success, huge popularity, and star status for everyone involved.

Some people spend an inordinate amount of time either desperately trying to avoid failure or covering up failure when it does occur (and it always does). Successful and confident people have learned that failure is an inevitable part of growth and life. Confident people embrace their failures as learning experience and strive to develop the conviction to do better the next time.

Again, it is like watching a boxing match. Some fighters who have been knocked down do not get back up, while another boxer who may have gotten just as devastating a blow will struggle to get up off the mat and often can turn the results of the match around. While the power of the blow can make some difference, I suspect that it is the power of the mindset and body of the person who got hit that is even more crucial. Interestingly, these are the two things that the boxer who got knocked down has the most control over. He can control (over time) how well he conditions his body to take these blows. Also, he can control his belief in his ability to turn around the fight and his tenacity to never give up. The boxer who is completely convinced that he should win the bout is surprised when he gets knocked down, but stays free from doubt. This self-confidence gets him to stand back up even when he is hurting. He may try to buy some time by staying down until the end of the count or by draping himself around the other player, but these methods are just used to create the opportunity to win.

So have you been taken down to the mat? Have you hit some rough spots in your career or life? In some ways you will be *better off* if you have. I liken it to the analogy of the water pistol game at the amusement park. If you have ever played this game then you know that the goal is to spray the water into the mouth of the clown, which will blow up the balloon on the top of the clown's head with air. The first player to aim well enough and get the balloon to burst wins the game. Then the attendant puts a new balloon on the clown's head where the previous balloon just burst and new players are invited to the game.

So, imagine that you are standing in line and the game was just completed. You have the option of sitting in chair #1 or chair #2. The winner of the previous game had been in chair #1 so they just put a brand new balloon on the clown's head. For chair #2, the balloon that had been inflated by the previous game, but did not burst, now goes down to its deflated shape and can be used again for this game. So, if you want to win this game and both water pistols are just as accurate, which chair are you going to sit in?

In my seminars, most people choose seat #2 reasoning that the balloon was already strained and thus should be easier to burst in the next game. However, the exact opposite is true. To increase your chances of winning the game you should absolutely sit in chair #1 with the new balloon. This balloon has never been stretched out before. Therefore, it is less capable of handling stress than the balloon that was previously stretched. The unstretched balloon will burst much faster than the one that has already been through a little trauma.

Do you believe that about life? If not, then why not? If you have been through a lot, then instead of thinking with a limit mentality of "I can't take one more thing," you might be better served to feel stretch and strengthened by your experiences. Perhaps the mindset should be, "I have proven myself to be a tough cookie. I can handle what comes my way." Of course, the ironic twist is whichever you believe, you are likely right.

THE ASSIGNMENT: Strength Through Adversity

What is the biggest challenge that you have faced and overcome in life? Think about this challenge as you answer the following questions:

1. The biggest challenge I've overcome is _____

    _____

2. My greatest learning from the experience was

    _____

    _____

3. One great thing in me or my life that would not have occurred if not for this experience is _____

    _____

    _____

THE
CONFIDENCE DRIVE

What lies behind us and what lies before us are tiny matters compared to what lies within us.

—Ralph Waldo Emerson

THE RESEARCH: Automobile Accidents

Have you ever been in an automobile accident? If you have, then you know that an accident can shake you up pretty badly. In fact, most people have a tough time getting back into a car the first time after a bad accident. When I first started driving, I (like many of you) was a nervous wreck. I mean the number of things that you had to pay attention to were staggering. Look ahead and make sure you are in the lines, check your rearview mirror, check your side view, look at the speedometer, and more. And at 16, I didn't even have to juggle a cell phone like drivers learning today. I mean, an automobile can cause a lot of destruction and accidents are not uncommon.

According to the US Department of Transportation, most drivers will have a "close call" in their cars around one to two times a month. They also report that the vast majority of individuals will be in an automobile collision on average every six years. Obviously, we need to take the responsibility of driving very seriously. In this chapter I would like to use the analogy of driving to represent a few lessons that are important for all of us to understand to navigate the journey of confidence.

THE APPLICATION

I'd like to draw an analogy between driving and life by looking at three things that we have to pay attention to when driving:
- The rearview mirror
- The side mirrors
- Our blind spots

When driving it is very important to occasionally check your rearview mirror. By knowing what is behind us, we are able to avoid potential dangers. We are able to stay ahead of trouble or get out of the way if it is coming too fast. However, a good driver cannot afford to overly focus on what is in the rearview mirror. A driver who attends too much to the rearview mirror at the expense of looking at the road ahead would most likely crash. The rearview mirror is there to glance at and be aware of what is behind you. It is not there to be the driver's primary focus.

Isn't life the same way? Let's say that what we see in the rearview mirror symbolizes our past. The person who *never* looks at or checks into his past is doomed to repeat mistakes and to be unaware of lurking dangers. However, the person who focuses too much on the past may completely miss present possibilities. We cannot see current and future opportunities when we keep replaying the past. Some people replay all of the harms that others have done to them. Others replay their own mistakes and flaws. Both are equally dangerous to one's confidence and ability to create a fulfilling life. The person who refuses to look at her past is also in danger. If you cannot embrace your past then you give it greater power over negatively impacting your future and your confidence.

Truly optimistic and confident people embrace their past, acknowledge its reality, mourn the pain, celebrate the success, learn from everything, and then focus on creating the present and future that they want. Of course, this is not an easy task or one done quickly, but it is a daily decision that gets easier when you refuse to run from your life and take full responsibility to pursue your dreams. Therefore, if you want to grow your confidence the first step is to fully look in the rearview mirror and do these steps.

But danger can come from other places. That is why we have side view mirrors in our cars. A speeding car may be coming up quickly beside us and we need that information to know if we can change lanes or maybe even give more room for someone to pass. I equate the side view mirror to those things that are going on in our life in the present day. We must be aware of our present day circumstances in order to maximize our ability to shift quickly to a new opportunity when it arises. We have to take an honest assessment of our current habits and behaviors that are either moving us toward or away from being the person we want to become. What habits do you have today that build your confidence? What habits do you have that take your confidence away?

However, again we cannot solely stay focused on what we are doing today. I've known many people that have the "great" ability to criticize themselves on a daily basis. They know what they are doing wrong. They know the things that are hurting them. However, they do penance by shaming themselves and then fail to change the behavior. Few things build confidence better than breaking free of a behavior pattern or habit that has been holding you back. But that takes combining what you currently see in your life with having a vision for a better way.

The blind spot is that area between what you can see in your mirrors and what exists around you. In order to view your blind spot while driving you have to take a special look beyond just checking your mirrors from your natural angle. How many people do you know that have a blind spot when it comes to seeing themselves in an honest light? Truthfully, we all have blind spots. Face it; most of us have lived with ourselves for all of our lives! Yet there are just some things that we don't realize about ourselves.

One night my brother Ken took me to a karaoke bar and there was a woman on stage named Jodie who was belting out Pat Benatar's "Hit Me with Your Best Shot." Now, when I say belting out, I am harkening back to my childhood discipline days when my father would take a belt to me. In other words, it was painful, seemed to go on forever, and I was almost sure it was never going to stop. Yes, Jodie was that bad. This was a fact that was apparently evident to everyone at the bowling alley with the exception of one person...Jodie. She seemed serious and intent and was obviously living in her own world at the moment (but it was OK because they know her there).

After Jodie finished I summoned up the courage to go up on stage myself and did Lionel Richie's "Still" (hey, I never said I was a cool karaoke singer). Afterwards, I started heading back to my seat when Jodie came up to me and said, "You were really good." So, what do you say in a situation like this? "Uh, thanks Jodie, your singing reminded my of the torture that souls must endure in the fifth concentric circle of Dante's hell," came to mind, but I decided that this level of truthfulness would not be an act of human kindness. So with some hesitation, I found the only truthful and kind statement that I could generate, "Uh, well you...you are really confident up there; yah, you carry yourself with a lot of confidence." But the main point of this story is Jodie's response. She replied, "Thanks, my secret is that I have my own karaoke machine at home. If I hear a note or two that I don't like I go back home and practice until I perfect the song." Ladies and gentleman, Jodie was clueless to the sound of her own voice. Jodie had a blind spot.

Looking in your blind spot (i.e., subconscious tendencies) requires help from those around you who can see things about you that you are blind to. People with lower confidence find this type of observation and feedback threatening. People who are confident or are dedicated to building their confidence yearn for and heartily welcome this type of feedback. To grow our confidence we must surround ourselves with people who will give us feedback into areas we may not see in ourselves. Then we can make a conscious decision about the behavior. However, it is impossible to make this conscious decision if we don't see the behavior.

So, as top-notch drivers, we check our rearview mirror for those things behind us, we check our side view mirrors for those things going on in the moment, and we check our blind spots for things we cannot readily see. Having taken these precautions we can now focus on the road ahead. As optimistic and confident people we know our past, see our current habits, know our strengths and weaknesses, and then keep our primary focus on where we are going and how we are going to get there.

THE ASSIGNMENT

Answer the following questions or do the following activities to prepare for your confidence journey:

Rearview mirror question:
What must you embrace (or mourn) from your past in order to allow yourself to be incredibly successful?

_____

_____

_____

Side view mirror question:
How are the people surrounding you in your life right now
impacting your confidence?

_____

_____

_____

Blind spot question:
Ask someone you trust to tell you what he or she thinks are
your biggest blind spots in terms of your strengths and/or
weaknesses.

_____

_____

_____

1.6

A HOLISTIC APPROACH TO UPGRADING YOUR CONFIDENCE

Confidence is courage at ease.

—Daniel Maher

THE RESEARCH: COPPING AN ATTITUDE

When someone says, "change your attitude" most of us think of this as a mental task. However, according to psychologists attitudes are actually formed and maintained by three components. The three components are:

- **Cognitive** (what we think)
- **Affective** (how we feel)
- **Behavioral** (what we do)

In other words, we can impact our attitudes in any of these three ways. My thoughts can impact my attitude about something, but so can my actions and my feelings. Let's use the example of heading up a high-profile team project for the first time. Initially, you may feel hesitant or slightly insecure about the role. However, think about how these three elements might impact your attitude about the new role.

1. You talk to yourself and remind yourself of your abilities and success up to this point. You bring into your mind that the CEO of the company believes in your ability and also knows that you won't do it perfectly the first time out of the gate. You also purchase books on project management and team leadership to learn techniques to help you in your position. You remind yourself that you will be proud of yourself after you do it (cognitive approach).

2. After proper preparation you make sure that you take time over the weekend (before the first meeting) to relax. You spend time laughing with friends. You take your spouse out to dinner and a movie and have a romantic evening. You even watch reruns of Friends or some other comedy over the weekend, which always put you in a good mood (affective approach).

3. You practice your approach to the meeting over the weekend. You give your presentation in front of the mirror to build your confidence in your presence and timing. You role-play potential scenarios with a friend in order to problem solve potential issues that might develop in the meeting (behavioral approach).

Any of these three could impact your attitude about heading up that new team project. Of course, a combination of the three would likely be even better.

Reference: Schwarz & Bohner, 2001.

THE APPLICATION

Many confidence books merely focus on how we think as the solution for building greater confidence. While these thinking strategies are useful and will be covered more in subsequent sections of this book, we must not forget the many other paths to greater confidence. These other paths include:

- Mental (our thoughts and mindsets)
- Emotional (our feelings)
- Behavioral (our actions)
- Relational (our community or relationships)
- Spiritual (our beliefs and purpose)

As you can see, this replicates the three factors that make up attitudes and then adds two additional factors. All five of these approaches can help free us from doubt and build our confidence to compete, perform or succeed well.

We are most content when what we believe, how we feel, and what we do are in harmony with one another. When all of these factors match we have the most internal peace and confidence. When they do not match, we have internal tension. This book will help you upgrade your confidence by looking at these five approaches one at a time. We will look at thinking strategies, feeling strategies, action strategies, relational strategies, and finally spiritual strategies to take your confidence to the next level.

THE ASSIGNMENT

You likely have a default method of approaching your confidence. Take the following informal test to determine if you have a preferred method of addressing confidence. For each statement, rank the answers. Put a five for the answer that best represents your opinion, a four for the next matching answer, and so on, until you finally put a one for the answer that represents your opinion the least: for now, ignore the letters next to the space in which you put your rating. We will use those later for scoring.

1. I can best tell that I am confident by:

What I believe about myself	____ (M)
How I feel about myself	____ (E)
My actions	____ (B)
Others' reactions around me	____ (R)
How connected I am with my mission	____ (S)

2. Truly optimistic and confident people:

Know it	____ (M)
Feel it	____ (E)
Act it	____ (B)
Relate it	____ (R)
Live it	____ (S)

3. The thing that can have the biggest impact on my confidence is:

What I say to myself	____ (M)
How I feel	____ (E)
What I do	____ (B)
How others treat me	____ (R)
The clarity of my purpose on this planet	____ (S)

4. I can tell others' level of confidence by how they:

Describe themselves	____ (M)
Show their feelings	____ (E)
Act	____ (B)
Relate to others	____ (R)
Live their beliefs	____ (S)

5. When my confidence is down I boost it by:

Using positive self-talk	____ (M)
Doing something to put me in a good mood	____ (E)
Accomplish a goal	____ (B)
Talk with someone who builds me up or cares	____ (R)
Praying or meditating on things important to me	____ (S)

6. I can tell that my confidence is falling by:

What I believe about myself	____ (M)
How I feel about myself	____ (E)
By my actions	____ (B)
By others' reactions around me	____ (R)
Because I am connected with my mission	____ (S)

7. Truly confident people:

Are positive thinkers	____ (M)
Feel great about themselves	____ (E)
Are results oriented	____ (B)
Surround themselves with supportive people	____ (R)
Have a focused purpose and mission	____ (S)

8. I can tell when people lack confidence because they:

Criticize themselves	____ (M)
Feel terrible about themselves	____ (E)
Act inferior	____ (B)
Are overly hurt by what others say and do	____ (R)
Have no sense of purpose	____ (S)

9. On my most confident day ever, I…

Knew it	____ (M)
Felt it	____ (E)
Showed it in my actions	____ (B)
Was supported by those around me	____ (R)
Had an incredible sense of purpose	____ (S)

10. The most effective strategy for me to improve my confidence is to:

Focus how I am talking to myself   _____ (M)

Focus on my emotions   _____ (E)

Focus on my goals and actions   _____ (B)

Surround myself with the right people   _____ (R)

Connect with something bigger than myself   _____ (S)

Now add up all of the letters:

Total number for M: _____

Total number for E: _____

Total number for B: _____

Total number for R: _____

Total number for S: _____

Key:

M = **Mental** or thinking approaches to confidence

E = **Emotional** or feeling approaches to confidence

B = **Behavioral** or action approaches to confidence

R = **Relational** or community approaches to confidence

S = **Spiritual** or life purpose approaches to confidence

The highest number or numbers represent your preferred method of dealing with confidence. This is likely either your best-developed method for confidence or just the one that you are drawn to the most. Your lower score might represent neglected paths to building your confidence. To maximize your effectiveness, you want to utilize all five paths to some degree.

MOTIVATION TO UPGRADE YOUR CONFIDENCE

Case Study

Tom was an up-and-coming key employee in a major Fortune 100 company. I was contacted by the Director of Human Resources and asked to meet with Tom for an initial session. The H.R. Director said that she was baffled by Tom's recent behavior. He had been a stellar performer who had recently been promoted from the field to become the manager of the sales department. In a short period of time they started seeing a different side of Tom. He had always been so incredibly confident as a salesperson and that is why they were shocked to see a series of behaviors that were new for Tom. In the field he was a model of efficiency. He was their top salesperson who was fearless as he went after new accounts. He would size up any challenge quickly and create a solution that would almost always end with success and profit. However, in his new role he seemed indecisive. In fact, he seemed to swing from passive, in terms of giving his team little direction, to aggressive and full of blame when the team did not get the results that he wanted. The company had recently gotten feedback from Tom's team that they were demoralized and tired of being bullied by this once-admired performer. Tom's boss had suggested that Tom take a course on managing people, which Tom had procrastinated doing for four months before blatantly refusing to do it because it would be "a waste of time." The company valued Tom greatly, but they were getting frustrated and concerned with his behavior and were considering letting him go. It was a classic case of someone being gifted as a producer who was promoted into a job that threw him off of his game.

When I met with Tom he was quite reserved and defensive. I could tell that he wasn't thrilled about meeting with me and didn't see the value of the two of us discussing the situation. He felt like H.R. was interfering with his job and they just needed to leave him alone to get the job done. Fortunately, I was able to get him to start opening up by talking about past successes that he had experienced as a salesperson. I wanted to get a sense of his strengths to see if we could tap into these to solve the current challenge. One strength that became apparent was his high sense of integrity. He considered himself an extremely responsible individual who had to have a strong impact on his company in order to feel good about his day. As I asked him to describe the impact that he was having as a sales manager for his company, his pride turned to anger. "It's not my issue. They have saddled me with a lazy team and I'm tempted to just fire all of them and start over again!"

Many individuals (men especially) express anger when really they are feeling something else beneath the anger. After some significant questioning and reflection Tom was able to admit to himself that beneath his anger was a feeling of shame about his performance. "As a salesperson I had no doubts. I knew exactly what I was doing and no one could tell me differently." Then with self-doubt flowing in his words he said, "But as a manager, I'm not creating the results I used to. I mean, no one had to tell me what to do when I was in the field; I just did it! But the people on my team aren't doing it. So I get on them, but that just got me in this situation. I just can't get them moving. Maybe I don't belong here. I'm just not confident I have what it takes to be an effective manager."

So now we were getting somewhere. In this type of situation someone like Tom has several choices. He could leave the company and look for a different position. He could see if he could continue to work with the company in a different capacity (maybe even back in his old position). He could do nothing and let the company decide his future. Or he could work to build his confidence in his current position (which would involve both his mental attitude and skill building). I asked Tom his thoughts on each of these options using questions that help clarify motivations and blocks. These questions and Tom's answers can be found in table 1.7A.

Table 1.7A

	What would motivate me to do this? How does it serve me to do it? What do I gain by doing it?	What would stop me from doing this? How does it hurt me to do it? What do I lose by doing it?
Choice A: Leave the company	❏ Get out of a bad situation ❏ Get to feel successful again ❏ Easy option	❏ Leave on a failure ❏ Hurts my reputation ❏ I like my company
Choice B: Go back to my old position	❏ I'd be successful ❏ I love the work ❏ I wouldn't have to manage others ❏ I'd have greater control over my success	❏ Feels like I'm going backwards ❏ Not challenging ❏ Less money ❏ Might lose respect from others
Choice C: Do nothing	❏ Easy option ❏ Don't have to admit that I am struggling	❏ Puts control of my future in others' hands ❏ Continue to feel no impact ❏ Have people upset with me ❏ It is not my personality to be passive
Choice D: Build my confidence as a manager	❏ Would feel like I am being responsible ❏ I want to do better ❏ I would feel great if I overcame this challenge ❏ I have a better future with this company ❏ I would make more money ❏ I'd show them I can do it	❏ Have to admit that I am not doing well ❏ Not sure I want this position ❏ What if it doesn't work?

Having all of these competing motivations in his head was slowing Tom down and contributing to his lack of success. By walking through his motivations with me, Tom was able to make a choice. He saw the positives of trying to build his confidence as a manager and realized that if that approach did not work, he could likely go back to being a salesperson. However, by trying to be successful as a manager he would at least have the pride of knowing that he attempted to do his best. This was important for his own sense of integrity. The option of doing nothing became very distasteful once he got it out in the open and the option of leaving the company did not appeal to him either. So Tom swallowed his "false pride" (having been unable to admit to his challenges) and connected with his healthy pride (wanting to give it his best shot) and agreed to coach and train with me.

While it took hard work and much tenacity, Tom is now seen as a true mentor in his company. He is viewed as an inspirational leader who is incredibly knowledgeable about the company, about how to sell difficult accounts, and about how to bring out the best in people. He is happy again and when we last talked it looked like another promotion was just around the corner.

The Challenge

To succeed, Tom had to be fully motivated toward his goal. If you have gotten this far in your reading then you have demonstrated your commitment to read this book. In addition to reading, I hope that you are fully committed to do all of the exercises. We are about to start exploring the five paths to confidence and I cannot emphasize enough the importance of doing the exercises along with the reading.

The real power in growing your confidence will come from these actions. For example, in the previous chapters we talked about the following techniques:

- Using the confidence balance wheel
- Resetting your internal thermostat
- Learning from adversity
- Using the automobile analogy to keep your percentage of focus in the most effective places
- Learning which confidence approach works best for you

At the end of later sections you will be asked to pick the best techniques from the ones that you tried in that particular section. However, the exercises that you have gone through in this section are all self-contained. If you have not completed them yet, I encourage you to go back and do so before continuing.

Do you believe that confidence can give you that competitive advantage or help you succeed better at your goals? Do you see how freedom from doubt can help you live a successful life with happiness for yourself and blessings for those around you? Are you motivated to take your confidence to the next level? If you feel completely motivated to do the confidence-building exercises in each of the five following sections (i.e., mental, emotional, behavioral, relational, and spiritual approaches to confidence) then skip the rest of this chapter and go on to chapter 2.1. If you have any doubts about your motivation to fully use this book then complete the following motivational chart (similar to the one Tom used). This will bring your competing thoughts and desires to the point of conscious decision.

	What would motivate me to do this? How does it serve me to do it? What do I gain by doing it?	What would stop me from doing this? How does it hurt me to do it? What do I lose by doing it?
Choice A: Read through this book quickly with-out doing the exercises	• _____ • _____ • _____ • _____	• _____ • _____ • _____ • _____
Choice B: Commit to six weeks (or whatever your pace is) of fully engaging with the material in this book	• _____ • _____ • _____ • _____	• _____ • _____ • _____ • _____

Congratulations! By completing this chart you are now able to make a conscious decision about what you are going to do! If you have struggled doing the exercises up to this point, then call a friend and ask him or her to walk through the book with you. This way you will be more diligent with the assignments and your friend will ben-efit also. Now let's go on to explore mental approaches to building your confidence.

SECTION 2

MENTAL STRATEGIES:

BELIEFS THAT LEAD TO PEAK PERFORMANCE

GET READY TO FULLY BELIEVE IN YOURSELF

It Makes You Wonder

I have a tendency to get myself in awkward situations. I mean, I don't try to, they just seem to present themselves to me with a high rate of frequency. On one such occasion I had taken my family to one of these indoor water parks. If you have never been to one of these, they can be quite fun. One very interesting invention that they have is the indoor wave pool. Now, you wouldn't think that you can get into too much trouble at a wave pool, but then again you don't expect to see what I saw at the pool either. I was out in the waves minding my own business in my large inner tube. As I casually paddled through the waves I noticed a woman having a wonderful time jumping up and down in the waves. The first thing I noticed was that the woman seemed very confident. She was a larger woman, but that didn't stop her from playing and frolicking with abandon in this swimming pool. Being someone who can be somewhat self-conscious about my weight I was suitably impressed. However, the second thing that I noticed immediately was that she had lost her bikini top.

So what do you do in a situation like this? Here I see this topless woman jumping about in the waves completely oblivious to the fact that she is making a spectacle of herself. I look around and no one seemed to have noticed yet. So being the kind and compassionate human being that I am I started paddling over to her to inform her of her precarious situation. As I paddled closer to her I kept rehearsing how I would break the news to her. "Um, excuse me miss, I don't know if you noticed a slight breeze or not, but it is probably because you lost your top" was one of the many lines I rehearsed trying to find the best way to communicate this to her without extremely embarrassing both of us. However, as I got closer, I chickened out. I just couldn't do it! So I started paddling toward the shore to get my wife to help this poor woman out (who still had not noticed that she was topless). I informed my wife Marla of the situation, but being shy by nature she informed me that there was no way in the world that she was going to swim out and tell this woman to get dressed. "She will figure it out soon" was her solution.

Then, the waves stopped. The water settled and now there was absolutely no way for this woman not to notice that she had half a swimming suit on. The woman started walking out of the water and amazingly she still did not notice her problem. So I told Marla that it was just cruel for us to watch this and do nothing. So I started to walk toward her. As the topless female got to knee-deep water I notice something very significant about her. "She" was a man.

Now, it is true that neither Marla nor I had our contacts in at the time, but for days all I could imagine was the number of bruises I would have gotten on my face if I had walked up to this gentleman and said, "Miss, I don't think you have realized this, but you have lost your top."

The Lesson

The way we view a situation can have serious ramifications. Our perceptions will often dictate what we do, how we feel, and how we interact with others. I had a solid perception that this man was a woman and perceived a problem in the situation. There was no problem in the situation. The entire problem was in my perception. Your mental framework or perceptions will impact your confidence. Doubts flow from poor perceptions and doubt can be poison to your success in business, in sports, or in life.

The Preview

These chapters we will explore the most popular way to build confidence: mental or cognitive strategies. In the following six chapters we will:
- Learn techniques for stopping "mind traffic"
- Explore an approach for taking control of our thoughts
- Look at the role of self-fulfilling prophecy in success and confidence
- Learn a simple and effective strategy for stopping unwanted thoughts (that will seem too easy to work, but it does)
- Build affirmations to upgrade your confidence
- Summarize and apply these mental strategies to your life

DE-CLUTTERING YOUR HEAD

The man who acquires the ability to take full possession of his own mind may take possession of anything else to which he is justly entitled.

—Andrew Carnegie

THE RESEARCH: Clearing our minds

Meditation can encompass anything from yoga to prayer and is misunderstood by many individuals. Basically, the person meditating is attempting to divert her focus in a way that allows her to be caught up in the present rather than the past or the future. Most Western meditation techniques involve focusing on an item or word until you empty your mind of all concerns. For example, a person may focus on the word "peace" and keep repeating it over and over until he achieves a feeling of being at peace. Or someone may meditate on a certain passage of scripture to fully embrace the meaning and message. In contrast, many Eastern meditation techniques focus on expanding your consciousness in a way that focuses on everything without thought or judgment.

Religions of all kinds have promoted the benefits of meditation to grow closer to God and to become more centered as a person. It is a way to drown out all of the chaos going on in our lives and focus on the things in life that have the most meaning to us. Research indicates that people who meditate show increases in self-esteem, openness, and general mental health.

References: Janowiak & Hackman, 1994; Sakairi, 1992.

THE APPLICATION

Being a perfectionist by nature, Steve always liked getting an early flight to make sure that he would be plenty early for his appointments. This particular appointment was a very important one for the software company he represented. Steve had been prepared by his boss that the clients were unhappy with some of the support they had gotten from the company in the last year and were also concerned that they did not have the most advanced product on the market. Although they had been working with Steve's company for years they were now having meetings with Steve's main competitor and it looked possible that they might lose the account. Steve was there to introduce recent advances to their product as well as address their service issues.

In the meeting, things were initially going fairly well. Steve felt confident of his presentation and the clients were asking the right questions at the right times and seemed pleased with his responses. There were a few points of tension, but for the most part Steve felt optimistic that he was going to keep this very important account. However, at one point in the meeting someone's cell phone went off. It kept ringing and ringing and everyone was looking around to see whose phone it was. This particular client group had a CEO who had a pet peeve about cell phones going off during meetings. In fact, the CEO even griped, "Haven't I told you all to keep those things off in these meetings? Whoever has the ringing phone, get rid of it." As the phone kept ringing, Steve realized that it was his. Being the perfectionist he was, he was very upset that he had forgotten to turn off his phone. He apologetically reached down to his bag to turn it off, but because of multiple embarrassing thoughts racing in his head he merely hung up on the caller without powering down. Sure enough twenty seconds later that phone started ringing again. Feeling completely mortified, Steve quickly shut off the phone and apologized. However, he could see from the look on the CEO's face that he had definitely lost ground by annoying him.

Steve's mind started racing and his composure started slipping. He forgot where he was at in his presentation and started repeating a point that he had already covered. He noticed the CEO shifting in his chair and looking even more annoyed. Steve started thinking about how dissatisfied his boss would be if he blew the account. His mind then went back to the account that he had lost several months ago as he started remembering how the meeting shifted from positive to negative just like this one was starting to do. Slowly Steve's previous confidence started falling like a series of dominoes that keep knocking each other down. Fortunately, one of the executives who was a big supporter of Steve's asked for a quick break during which Steve was able to regain his composure and get back in and win back the account.

Our minds are capable of processing a huge amount of information. This is both a plus and a minus concerning whether this information aids us or hurts us. What goes on in our minds has a powerful impact on our confidence and our behavior. Having the wrong stuff in our heads is dangerous to our success. Some people have minds that work like a one-lane country road; others have mental activity that more closely parallels a sixteen-lane freeway with cars driving way over the speed limit. I suspect that most of us fall closer to that second category. If you do, it is very important to gain control of what is going on in your mind. Later in this book I will teach you a very specific technique to stop unwanted thoughts; in this chapter I want to focus more on the need to slow down your day, your thoughts, and your spirit to make sure that nothing is flying around in your head that shouldn't be there.

What is more likely to fill your mind: the past, the present, or the future? Some people live in the past. They are always talking about past relationships, past accomplishments, or worse yet all of the past hurts or pains they have experienced. Others live in the future and are always hoping for something they might have. "I would be happy if I only had _____" might be the motto. Or they worry about the future and what might or might not happen. Obviously, it is good to learn from the past (or even heal from it) and to have future goals and dreams. However, if the past and future make up too many lanes in our mental highway then we might miss living in today's moment. I am at my most content when I can find pleasure in even the simplest moments in my present life. Too much of a focus on the past or the future interferes with my confidence today. We must balance all three of these.

Can you be optimistic, confident and content even in this moment of reading this book? Can you celebrate who you are today, not just who you might be tomorrow? Can you be confident that no matter what your past, you are the captain of your life today? Living in the present moment is crucial to the confident person.

One moment I love from the movie *Lost in Translation* is when the Bill Murray character is doing karaoke and is singing the Bryan Ferry song, "More Than This." What he communicates to the woman he is singing to is that the very moment that they are experiencing is wonderful and perfect and complete, that "there is nothing more than this." It is a moving moment that motivated me to go out and buy a CD with that song on it. Every now and then I need to pull out that song. When I'm running to the airport again and too focused on the future (worrying "When will I get there," "How will it go," "What's on my schedule next week") it is good to put in the CD and relax my spirit and simply enjoy the car ride to Chicago's O'Hare airport. When I do this, I change my focus to what I am doing in that moment, I start appreciating the fact I am alive and I allow myself to fully experience my present. And believe it or not, sometimes I really feel like there is nothing "More Than This."

THE ASSIGNMENT

Find a style of meditation or prayer that works for you, and do it for ten minutes. The purpose of this exercise is to focus your attention away from the past and the future and keep it focused on the present moment. You can meditate by simply picking a word to repeat over and over while you sit in a quite place like "peace," "tranquility" or "yes." You could focus on a pray of thanks such as "Thank you God for _____," repeating this over and over for things in your present life. Or you could read scripture and meditate on the meaning for your life. If you are uncomfortable with these approaches, find a more secular form of being in the moment, such as really studying your morning tea, juice, or coffee. Allow yourself to experience in the moment all the nuances of taste, temperature, aroma, and texture. Stay in that moment and simply be grateful for the simple pleasure of your morning beverage. Silly? The people experiencing less stress and greater health don't think so!

Never build a case against yourself.

—Norman Vincent Peale

THE RESEARCH: How We Form Conclusions

How do we go about forming our opinions and beliefs? Given how important our perceptions are to our actions and success, it is crucial to understand how these develop. I'd like to share two findings from research related to forming conclusions. The first is research concerning the logic of mental arguments. Syllogisms are logical arguments based on several premises that lead to a conclusion. For example:

- People are good by nature
- Politicians are people
- Therefore, politicians are good by nature

Do you agree with this finding? How about this one:

• Women are not as assertive as men
• Martha Stewart is a woman
• Therefore, Martha Stewart is not as assertive as a man

Research shows that faulty judgment can occur due to misleading premises that are related in some way. Therefore, we must be very cautious about the premises we use to make decisions.

The second finding of note is the impact of rational-emotive behavior therapy. REBT is a form of therapy that addresses and helps replace self-defeating thoughts such as "I need to be loved by everyone to be worthwhile." Research has shown that revealing and changing these beliefs can lead to greater success, emotional stability and happiness. The approach, TruthTalk, discussed in this chapter, is based on this technique.

References: Ashcraft, 2002; Ellis, 1995.

THE APPLICATION

When I was about eleven, I had an early morning paper route that started just as the sun was coming out. One morning I heard a mechanical sound that I had never heard before. I looked around and couldn't find anything that could account for the noise that I heard. Then I saw it—the UFO. I could barely make it out. It was high in the sky and it seemed to have on some sort of cloaking device because I could only see the dark edges; the rest was invisible. I quickly ran over to the next block and found my best friend who was also getting ready to go out on his route. After a quick explanation he and I agreed that we needed help so we ran to my house to wake my parents. Now, you probably have to be a son of a minister to get this type of response, but when I told my father about the flying saucer he rolled back over in bed and quoted some verse from the Bible about "seeing strange things in the end times." Obviously, he was going to be of no help in the coming invasion. I did manage, however, to wake up my brother who joined us. So three young boys armed with our BB guns and the few firecrackers that we could gather went to stop the alien horde.

We looked around and didn't see anything, but I told them that the UFO had a cloaking device on so we would have to listen for the sound (obviously their science gave them the ability to mask sight, but was not advanced enough to develop a quiet engine). Soon we heard the sound and sure enough, up in the sky was the dark outline of the alien vessel. My friend yelled when he saw it saying, "It's really true; aliens are attacking." He then went diving behind a parked car in fear. Realizing that my BB gun was unlikely to bring down the ship and was no match for the "death rays" that the aliens likely had, I decided to dive down next to him. "Get down," we yelled to my older brother who was just standing out in the open seemingly in shock from the sight of the UFO. Then he started laughing. "Tim, that's nothing but a flock of birds." And sure enough as my friend and I looked up with a different perspective, it was the outline of a flock of birds flying high above, and all of a sudden that high pitched "mechanical" noise sounded amazingly similar to birds chirping in unison.

Somehow I had managed to misperceive that entire situation. Even more amazing is that my friend's perception was also fooled because of the interpretation I suggested to him. Now you might say that this is just an example of an eleven-year-old with an overactive imagination, but the truth is that we misperceive things on a daily basis. Often we will get all upset and out of sorts over something that someone said, only to discover that we misperceived it. We form perceptions and beliefs that can impact our confidence and create a great deal of insecurity. Some common beliefs that can hold you back from your best confident self are:

- I must be perfect
- I must please others
- Everyone must love me
- Failure is terrible
- I *should* (fill in the blank) _____

These are not statements of fact. These are perceptions or beliefs that we form due to modeling from our past or our own insecurities. Parallels to these thoughts that are more truthful and more conducive to high confidence are:

- I will never be perfect so I embrace my humanness as I strive to do my best
- I like to please others, but it is more important to do the right thing
- It is great when others love me, but that has nothing to do with my worth
- Failure is part of living and I can learn from every mistake
- I *want* to (fill in the blank)_____

There are many techniques that deal with revealing your beliefs and aligning them with reality and performance rather than around insecurity and stagnation. The TruthTalk formula is a combination of several of these cognitive approaches and can help you align your thought process with thoughts that create confidence and success. With a little practice you can eliminate negative or performance-reducing thoughts and replace them with a mindset and attitude that will take you to your next level of confidence.

THE ASSIGNMENT

I teach several versions of TruthTalk, but for this assignment I am going to suggest a simple version that is helpful for catching mental patterns. Use the following series of questions to discover and impact your beliefs that impact your confidence.

Recall an event that recently challenged your confidence. Find one where the problem was due to a misread of the situation.

Step	My example	Your example
Step 1: Write only the facts about the event here (no interpretations).	*My boss sent me an email that we needed to talk urgently*	
Step 2: Write down how you felt.	*I felt worried*	
Step 3: Write down the perception that made you feel that way. What were you saying to yourself that caused the emotion?	*I must have done something wrong*	
Step 4: What would have been a more truthful, realistic or helpful perception to have at the time?	*I have no clue what she wants so I refuse to worry about it. It won't be anything I can't handle and may be something positive.*	

If you do a series of these, you will start noticing patterns in what kind of thoughts decrease your confidence. Once you see the pattern then you have more power to change it.

2.4

CHANGING THE SELF-FULFILLING PROPHECY

As is our confidence, so is our capacity.

—William Hazlitt

THE RESEARCH: What We Predict Often Comes True

A well-founded psychological theory is that once we form an opinion of someone else (or even ourselves) we can subconsciously enact behaviors that cause others or ourselves to conform to our expectations. For example, if I have a belief that I am a bad golfer and I make a great shot, I can almost guarantee that my next shot will be poor unless I change my belief about myself as a golfer. In other words, if deep down we do not feel confident in our ability to do something and we actually do that activity well, our subconscious will fix it to match expectations. This is called a self-fulfilling prophecy. ·

Maybe this is part of what explains the dramatic advantage optimistic people seem to have. Martin Seligman has spent decades studying optimism and pessimism. In his bestseller, *Learned Optimism: How to Change Your Mind and Your Life*, he shares how optimistic people:

- Get depressed less frequently than do pessimistic people
- Get elected to public office more often than do pessimistic people
- Commonly exceed the expectations of aptitude tests
- Excel in school and college
- Have unusually good health
- Age well and experience fewer physical ailments common in middle age
- May actually live longer than pessimists

Optimistic people believe that good things will happen for them. And guess what. This belief often creates a competitive edge in performance and in living a happy and fulfilling life.

References: Kenrick, Neuberg, & Cialdinin, 2002; Seligman, 1998.

THE APPLICATION

"I just know I'm not going to get the promotion," he said with a mixture of sadness and anger in his eyes. Jay was serious when he said this to me. Now, I knew that he was seriously being considered to become a senior manager in the company and I also knew that it was going to be a close call. "Jay, why in the world would you want to predict that?" I asked. "Wouldn't it be better to predict that you are worthy of promotion and that they will likely see it?" My concern was that Jay's lack of confidence in the likelihood of his promotion could actually hurt his chances of getting promoted. If he didn't think he should get promoted, why should they? I explained to Jay the principle of self-fulfilling prophecies and warned him of the impact this could have on his chances. Sadly, Jay refused to listen. He felt that it was more realistic to assume that he would not be disappointed. He justified this by saying that by keeping this expectation he could minimize his disappointment when the promotion failed to come through. Jay was predicting failure in order to protect himself.

Jay's pessimistic stance was like the person who shoots himself in the arm because one day armed robbers might come into his house to shoot him. It makes no sense, but it is a common tendency. Not surprisingly, Jay did not get the promotion. And while there is no way to guarantee that he would have gotten it if he believed it to be likely, I have no doubt that his stance of defeat did not aid him in his goals. By taking a stance that had the illusion of protection, Jay may have actually given up his true power and ability to protect and improve himself.

What are the pessimistic self-fulfilling prophecies that you may be subconsciously creating?

- "I'm stuck at this level in the company"
- "I could *never* (fill in the blank)"_____
- "Nothing will ever change in my marriage"
- "No one will ever give me the credit I deserve for this project"

Whatever the form of the prophecy, is it a prediction that you really want to make? What if you eliminated all negative self-prophecies and substituted them with optimistic ones like:

- "I am going to be promoted"
- "I *can* (fill in the blank)" _____
- "I can impact my marriage for the positive"
- "I will make sure that someone recognizes the work that I put in to this project"

The lesson? If you are going to make a prophecy, make sure it is one that benefits you! Optimistic and confident people have an uncanny ability to believe in their success. Whether or not they will succeed is never in question, it is just a matter of when!

THE ASSIGNMENT

Let's make some positive predictions for your future. Fill in the following blanks, but allow yourself to really dream and hope. Let's make these predictions using a one-year time frame.

In one year:

- I am going to accomplish _____
  _____

- I will definitely _____
  _____

- I will impact _____ by doing
  _____

- My greatest hope is that I will _____
  _____

THOUGHT-STOPPING

It's hard to fight an enemy who has outposts in your head.

—Sally Kempton

THE RESEARCH: Developing Mental Stop Signs

Thought-stopping is a structured procedure for eliminating trouble-some thoughts. It was popularized by Joseph Wolpe and has been used to treat a wide variety of challenges including:

- Obsessive thinking
- Need for assertiveness
- Phobic reactions
- Smoking cessation

Thought-stopping can be used alone or combined with other cognitive techniques such as TruthTalk. It also can be used to help someone focus on successful outcomes and build confidence. While the form of thought-stopping can vary, the basic procedure is:

1. Wear a rubber band on your wrist
2. Any time you have the undesirable thought, you snap the rubber band (not hard, just enough to feel it)
3. Visualize a stop sign or yell "stop" (unless you are in a grocery store or other public place)
4. Repeat to yourself a replacement thought that is more helpful
5. Rinse and repeat (well, just repeat)

The technique is meant to help "train the brain" to quit allowing the automatic and destructive thoughts. Since thoughts are intangible, the rubber band helps make the process more concrete. The process is simple and usually only takes a few days or weeks to feel a major impact.

Reference: Wolpe, 1973.

THE APPLICATION

When it comes to growing our confidence by controlling our thinking we need to look at both thoughts that we want to start thinking and those that we want to stop thinking. There are certain ingrained thoughts that we have that distract us from being our confident best.

These thoughts can come from various sources:
- Messages from childhood
- Self-doubt and criticism
- Fear of the future
- A previous boss who was unreasonable
- A critical spouse

We cannot control what others say to us, but we definitely can impact and change what we say to ourselves. Some people take pride in saying, "I am my own worst critic." That is not something to brag about; in fact when you think about it, the statement is kind of stupid. I mean you might as well go around saying, "Nope, it isn't others that hold my confidence back; I do that little number all by myself or at least I do it better than anyone else"! Doesn't make too much sense, does it?

Individuals who want to stop negative or fearful thoughts try all sorts of complex strategies for relief. In my years of working as a therapist and coach I have found thought-stopping to be one of the most effective, yet simple, strategies that psychology has to offer. For example, I was working with a very successful CEO who had difficulty firing people even when they were acting in a harmful fashion to others in the company. His thought process was, "If I fire him then I will have failed in some way." As messed up as this thought sounds, this highly successful business owner had it swimming around in his head and it was interfering with what was best for the company. He talked with me on multiple occasions about a particularly difficult employee who was hurting morale. In truth, he knew that it was far past time to let him go and now we had to focus on what was holding him back from canning this destructive individual. Once we discovered it was this failure thought, I taught the CEO the technique of thought-stopping. He decided to use, "I have given him multiple chances and it is the employee's failure to change, not mine, that is causing him to be fired" as his replacement thought.

Two weeks later in our next meeting the CEO informed me that the technique was not working. I looked at his wrist and noticed that there was no rubber band. "Where is the fancy thought-stopping apparatus I gave you?" I said jokingly. His response was, "Oh, I just did it in my head, and it didn't work." I then went on to reinforce the reason why I asked him specifically to use the rubber band and encouraged him to try it again. Within two weeks the employee was let go and the CEO felt no guilt whatsoever with it. When done right, thought-stopping can work wonders. Whether you want to quit smoking or build your confidence, this procedure is certainly something that is easy to add to your other techniques.

If you are plagued by any repeating thoughts that you would like to get rid of then there is no reason not to try this tactic.

THE ASSIGNMENT

Prepare yourself for the possibility of using thought-stopping as your technique of choice for this section. Do this by simply answering these first two questions:

1. Identify the thought that you want to stop. Write it here:

   _____

   _____

2. Identify a new thought that you would like to think about instead of the negative thought written above. Write the new thought here:

   _____

   _____

Consider the rest of these steps as your possible action plan as you finish up the section of this book on thinking techniques.

3. Wear a rubber band on your wrist and lightly snap it every time the negative thought occurs (remember it is a light snap so that your brain recognizes it as a stimulus, not a punishment to change your behavior)

4. When you snap, think "STOP" and then switch to your positive or helpful thought written above

5. Repeat this process as many times as it occurs for at least two weeks.

If you would like a free "Act Confident" rubberband, simply request one at www.advantagecoaching.com.

AFFIRMATIONS

*It's not who you are that holds you back,
it's who you think you're not.*

—Author unknown

THE RESEARCH: ...And Doggone it, People Like You

The research on self-concept suggests that how we view ourselves is highly related to positive feedback and affirmations received in childhood. Carl Rogers emphasized that we have a natural tendency to grow as human beings. This growth can be stifled if we experience intense critical evaluations. Rogers' style of helping people focuses on giving them positive feedback and affirmation with complete acceptance of the individual as a person. We would do well to practice this for ourselves. I have worked with too many people who are overly dependent on self-criticism to motivate themselves and who have never released themselves from the negative voices of parents or peers in their own head. If you don't love yourself (which is not the same as liking everything you do) then who will?

Reference: Rogers, 1961.

THE APPLICATION

When many people think of affirmations they seem to think of the old *Saturday Night Live* sketch with the motivational guru who looks in the mirror and says, "I'm good enough, I'm smart enough, and dog-gone it, people like me." While this sketch was hilarious, it has given a bad taste to self-affirmation. Some people view the concept of self-affirmation as "fluffy" or just for people with low self-esteem. What a ridiculous notion! Anyone who has played competitive sports knows that a negative mindset can crush your game and a positive mindset can enhance it. If you were coaching a young tennis player would you be yelling these things from the sideline?

- I can't believe you just missed that again!
- You are horrible!
- You might as well be wearing a blindfold if you are going to play like that!

Or might you be more effective coaching with statements like:

- You can get this!
- You are an incredible player so play up to your game!
- I know you can do it!

Obviously the player getting the second type of coaching will do better. So why should we treat our business game with fewer mental strategies than our sports game? Unless you are a professional athlete, your business game is your bread and butter and will have more impact on your life than your weekend golfing or baseball game. Our business confidence and performance (even if your business is being a stay-at-home parent) deserves our absolute best. We should be more disciplined in our mental game. We should be more intentional in our thinking. And we should use the science of positive affirmations to create confidence to handle any challenges.

Unfortunately, many top performers are not used to this type of a perspective. Many get to a certain level of success by being extremely driven and critical of themselves. This often relates to being brought up in a negative and critical home. I have observed many CEOs who were unable to grow their companies because they refused to change tactics. They had beat themselves up to get to where they were and they were going to continue to berate themselves and others in their company to get to the next level. Oh, they did not want coaching from me, they just wanted me to fix all the "lazy incompetents" they hired. The problem was that they could not get to the next level of success without changing tactics. Their critical mindsets did help them reach a certain level of success, but new challenges require new strategies. It was time to put away the old style of thinking and develop a new style. Only those who were willing to make this shift grew their companies. The others stagnated or ended up destroying all that they had built.

Utilizing affirmations is not fluffy or weak. There is a science at work here. And the research is clear that well-developed and rehearsed affirmations lead to happiness and success.

THE ASSIGNMENT

The first step to a thriving mindset is to gain awareness of your abilities and positive attributes. Answer the following questions with full confidence and honesty:

1. Something that I am exceptional at is:

   _____

   _____

2. I am proud that I:

   _____

   _____

3. One new accomplishment that I could make if I fully adopt a thriving mindset is:

   _____

   _____

APPLYING YOUR THINKING STRATEGIES

Case Study

Matt was on the fast track to success. I had been coaching Matt's boss and one of the things we were working on was having more effective team meetings. I first met Matt when I traveled out to Boston to observe one of these meetings.

Matt would sit silent in the team meetings, doodling on his notepad and making occasional exasperation noises when he didn't like something that was being said. Then every now and then Matt would pipe in loudly, almost verbally attacking his boss or coworkers for something they said. Despite this behavior Matt was a superstar and many times what he had to say contained great wisdom and insight. However, how he said it showed immaturity and was hurting his reputation. Matt's boss Karen asked me "How could a man as talented and capable as Matt be so disruptive and disrespectful? Doesn't he know I impact him getting promoted? You would think he would keep that in mind when he gives me feedback." She even started questioning whether it was the fact that she was a woman that made Matt so disrespectful. As she continued to wonder about that she became more and more angry and I could tell that Matt was getting under her skin. Something needed to change or Matt was going to lose his job and his boss was going to lose her star player.

Many times when I coach a team leader I meet with the different team members to get the different perspectives and an idea of the team dynamics. I will also often use an instrument from Inscape Publishing called the DiSC®, to assess the different team member styles and use it to help each team member understand potential strengths and challenges. I suggested to Matt's boss that I would like to try to work with him. Once we figured out the proper balance between in-person and over the phone coaching sessions, she gladly approved the request. However, she informed me that Matt was not a great coaching candidate and didn't want me to waste my time if he was not coachable. She did not seem to have much hope for success.

Matt was resistant at first, but I was soon able to get him to realize that I was there as an advocate for the team and was not there to make him into a bad guy. I also decided that the best way to deal with Matt was to be respectful, but very direct. We went over his DiSC® results, which objectively nailed his challenges. Some of the findings were that he created win-lose situations, was too blunt, ignored the people issues at times, and had a fear that others would take advantage of him. Fortunately, Matt was able to take the critique and asked if (as long as it could be confidential) we could use more coaching to work on these areas. With his boss's enthusiastic approval we continued.

Matt was a smart guy and very intellectual with his approach to his work (except when his feelings took over). Therefore, I took a thinking strategy with him initially. Now, you may be thinking "Matt appears to be very confident" and you would be right to a degree. However, I have found that behind almost any aggressive behavior is a lack of confidence of some sort. This turned out to be the case with Matt around the idea of others taking advantage of him. This scared him and caused him to see threats when none existed. In short, his extreme protection and emotional reactions indicated to me that he did not feel confident enough in his ability to either protect himself or survive someone taking advantage of him. He was hypervigilant out of fear of this happening.

A breakthrough came for Matt when we analyzed his thoughts using the TruthTalk formula. Through various events we revealed that Matt felt fear and anger over perceived threats to his career and performance and that these were exaggerated dramatically. When Matt saw this in black and white on paper he immediately committed to changing it. "That's just stupid," he said. Luckily, Matt was an ideal coachee and immediately put his insight into practice. Sure enough, he found the pattern was true. Every time he overreacted to something it was related to his level of perceived threat. His progress came through a combination of:

- Daily meditation to calm his hypervigilance
- A combination of thought-stopping, TruthTalk, and affirmations to transform his negative thinking of, "He's out to hurt me" to "Whatever comes up I can handle it"

- Role playing adaptive ways to handle himself in meetings and confront situations in a way that built his reputation rather than hurt it which helped him to predict success and make it happen

Matt checks in every now and then and is doing great. He got the new title he wanted as well as a nice raise and is now considered a low maintenance high performer instead of a high maintenance high performer. Matt loves the mental game of catching his thoughts and taking control of them. He sees it as almost a chess match between the rational and irrational parts of his mind. Basically, he has fun with it (despite not having to practice it nearly to the level he used to). He is confident of his ability to both protect himself and do it in a way that is mature, effective and inspirational to those around him.

The Challenge

Review the mental strategies presented in the five previous chapters. Which cognitive tactic or tactics seem most helpful to you?

- Meditation and/or prayer to de-clutter your mind
- TruthTalk to catch faulty perceptions and beliefs that threaten confidence
- Predicting success to increase your belief that you will succeed
- Thought-stopping to eliminate thoughts that drain confidence
- Affirmations to build your belief in yourself

Take at least one of these techniques (although several can be easily combined) and make a commitment to how you will apply it on a regular basis in your life. Write your commitment to yourself here:

I commit to _____

_____

_____

I will do this every _____

_____

_____

EMOTIONAL APPROACHES:

BUILDING DEEP CONFIDENCE THROUGH INSIGHTS AND FEELINGS

GET READY TO FEEL CONFIDENT

It Makes You Wonder

I am a most excellent driver (although I doubt you will believe me when you are done reading this section). Not only am I an exceptional driver, but I perform some of my best concerts while driving in the car. Sure, other people sing in the car (you might even be one of them), but I belt it out. In fact, singing in the car by myself is one of my great pleasures in life, second only to the great reverberation I get when I sing in the shower. I love singing in the car and despite the fact that every other person that I have seen singing in their car looks incredibly goofy, I am convinced in my mind that I somehow escape this common dilemma and look very cool.

So one day I was driving along and I was in my prime. I can't remember the song I was singing (although with my tastes it could have been anything from music from *Les Miserables* to Prince), but I do remember that I was in a great mood. The sun was shining, the birds were singing, and so was I. In fact, I was so engaged in my singing that when I came to a 4-way stop sign I was unsure whose turn it was so I started to pull out. Well, as I pulled out, so did the Ford Taurus to my right. We both had to quickly hit our brakes in order to avoid the collision. Still smiling, I turned to the other driver with my best "Whoops, that was a close one" facial expression and was met with a glare that wasn't what I would call warm and inviting. In fact, the gentleman driving the Taurus was yelling and swearing at me and making a gesture involving one of his five fingers that somehow has taken on a negative connotation in our culture.

Now I am a relatively mature man who has devoted himself to understanding the human psyche and trying to live a conscious life at peace with my fellow man. So how do you think I responded? Yep, I responded exactly the opposite of a mature man. My conscious mind gave way to an immediate emotional response. I matched the other person's aggressiveness, throwing up my arms in the air and giving the best "First day driving a car?" look that I could muster. After furiously waving him on, I continued to drive to work. However, I left my pleasant mood back at the stop sign. For about twenty minutes I thought about what a jerk this guy was and how ridiculous it is to treat another human being so poorly for a simple mistake at a stop sign. In other words, I gave this gentleman far more "head space" that he deserved and allowed the incident to distract me twenty minutes longer than it should have bothered me.

Later that week, a similar event occurred. Yes, once again I pulled out at the same time as another driver. So this time I am ready to rumble and I respond with the best "You want a piece of this" look I could muster, then squinting my eyes to communicate "Go ahead, make my day." To my surprise I was met by a woman's kind face which expressed something along the lines of "Oops, you go ahead," as she gestured me to take the lead. Well I quickly changed my expression to the same and said "Oh, no, no, no, no, you go" (although she had to read my lips to get the message). I drove away thinking how nice people are and how different it had been from my previous stop sign encounter.

Well, I believe that God was trying to teach me a lesson because believe it or not, within a day it happened again. This time it was an older gentleman behind the wheel of the other car. He was upset and let me know it through a variety of gestures. However, this time I chose to retain my own mood and simply gave him an "it's OK, go ahead" signal. I continued to drive on to work with my pleasant mood safely intact. I chose to be myself instead of letting my immediate emotions take over and cause me to betray myself by letting the other person control my mood and behaviors. I maintained my cool and maintained my confidence. The optimistic and confident individual does not allow other people to control his emotions so easily.

The Lesson

How many times have we looked at someone else's behavior and said, "That wasn't very logical"? The truth is that often our behaviors are not logical, but are ruled by our immediate emotional response. Daniel Goleman in his book *Emotional Intelligence* talks about the "emotional hijacking" that occurs in our brains. The amygdala is the part of our brain that instantly gauges the emotional significance of events. This triggering can be immediate and intense and is emotional in nature rather than logical. The problem is that many times our emotional response is not one that we would have chosen in hindsight.

If we add on to our driving analogy from chapter 1.5, our emotions would represent what we have playing on the radio. What is the soundtrack of your life? Do you have an inner melody of confidence, one of mediocrity or even worse, one of chaos or sadness? The best way to answer this question is to examine how you handle stress. Human beings are like cans of soda under stress. If you shake up the can enough and crack it open, whatever kind of soda that is in the can will come spraying out. What sprays out of you when you are going through tough times? Some people take on a victim mentality during challenges and simply talk about how others have done them wrong. Other individuals become angry and aggressive under stress and look to hurt others when they feel vulnerable. Still others lie down in the corner and cower before life, becoming paralyzed in the process (they are like those bugs that roll up when they sense threat—not the most effective defense mechanism in nature). In contrast, some people become incredibly goal-oriented and tenacious under stress. They focus on problem solving and are convinced that they will find a way to overcome the challenges even when the answers are not apparent to them at the moment. Yes, our behaviors under stress will reveal a lot about the soundtrack playing in our emotional lives.

Another way to gauge your emotional level of confidence is to examine your relationship to compliments. What do you do when someone compliments you? I've known people that have an amazing ability to deflect the most genuine of compliments.

"Oh, this old thing, I just threw it on."

"No, I just got lucky."

"Yes, I've lost a few pounds, but I have a long way to go."

"Anyone could have done it as well."

"I'm not really that smart, I just work really hard."

Some people simply ignore it when you compliment them and look, embarrassed, at the ground. On the other side of the continuum are the people who are desperate to get your compliment.

"No one has noticed my new outfit."

"Doesn't anyone recognize the hard work I put into this?"

"Can't anyone tell I've lost weight?"

"I wonder how they think I did in my presentation?"

"I'll show them how smart I am."

Some quietly suffer when they don't get complimented, while others are like deep sea fishermen casting out hooks of their accomplishments hoping someone will take the bait and let them reel in a compliment.

The optimistic and confident person can hear a compliment, embrace it, and thank the giver for it, but at the same time is not desperate to get it. The compliment is a wonderful fringe benefit rather than a sought-after Holy Grail. So what is your relationship to compliments? What do you think that tells you about your emotional confidence? How we handle stress and how we deal with compliments are just two windows into our inner life and confidence. The greater confidence we have, the more we will be in conscious control of what we feel and thus what we do.

While emotions can be difficult to control they are not impossible to impact. The trouble is that most people exclusively try to deal with emotions with words and self-talk strategies. Don't get me wrong; I believe in self-talk strategies (as you experienced in the last section). These techniques can be powerful and can help many people. The point, however, is that there are many other techniques that we can use to impact our confidence that go straight to our emotional world.

You see, words are man-made; we created them to communicate. Therefore, words do not always impact the more primal parts of our nature. Emotions are much more susceptible to things we see, noises we hear, things we smell, and other sensory events. The sight of a bear tearing through my home will frighten me immediately. I don't need to think, "Hmm, bears have big teeth, bears like to eat, a bear could eat me, there is a bear in my house, ergo, I am in danger." No, my fear is primal and instantaneous. At the same time, the sight of tree limbs swaying with the breeze can relax me. The smell of vanilla calms me. My wife can calm me quickly when I am frustrated with a simple touch on my arm. These things are independent of words. To impact your confidence at the deepest of levels you must be able to tap into this inner world of emotion. The following six chapters will help you do that.

The Preview

In the following six chapters we will focus on feeling or emotional strategies for building your confidence. Within this context we will:

- Learn techniques for gaining insight into your emotional core
- Look at the role of accountability in building emotional confidence
- Examine how we can impact our emotions using all of our senses
- Explore creative uses of music, art, and movies to change your level of confidence
- Introduce the powerful technique of neurolinguistic programming (NLP) to impact your emotional confidence
- Summarize and allow you a chance to choose the most powerful feeling strategies and set your strategy for feeling more confident

GAINING INSIGHT INTO YOUR UNSEEN WORLD

When there is no enemy within,
the enemies outside cannot hurt you.

—African Proverb

THE RESEARCH: WHY WE FEEL WHAT WE FEEL

There are three theories of emotion in psychology that I would like to share with you. A simple way to compare these theories is to take a situation in which you may have fear (i.e., seeing a rattlesnake) and letting the theories explain why you feel afraid.

James Lange theory: Centers on how our behavioral response to something creates our emotional experience of it. In other words, you are afraid of the snake because you run from it. This theory is focused on the relationship between our actions and our feelings.

Cannon-Bard theory: States that you are afraid because your brain (via the thalamus and the amygdala) interprets the snake as dangerous without much conscious thought. Therefore, emotions are automatic and primal rather than cognitively based. We don't have to think about being scared by a snake to be afraid of it.

Cognitive theory: States that you are afraid because of the way that you interpret the event of seeing a snake. In other words, you think of snakes being dangerous and therefore feel fear. Our emotions are caused by our thoughts or mental analysis of an event or object.

We could debate the merits of each of these theories or we could accept that there may be truth to each. Sometimes we feel a certain way because we behave a certain way. Other times our feelings are more primal and immediate. And still other times our feelings are due to our cognitive interpretation of what is going on around us. Either way, it is important for us to understand what we feel, why we feel it, and what we can do about it.

References: James, 1980; Anderson & Phelps, 2000; Lazarus, 1991.

THE APPLICATION

"How confident do you feel?" I asked him. "I think I am very confident" was his intriguing response. Did he really answer my question? I don't believe he did. You see, our emotions and our thoughts often walk hand-in-hand with each other. But just like a loving couple they occasionally have spats and go off to their opposite corners of the room. Sometimes they even move out and don't even live in the same neighborhood. Some people are aware of the differences they have in their *thoughts* about themselves and their *feelings* about themselves. However, others have not taken an adequate amount of time to really understand how they truly feel about themselves, their abilities and their confidence.

I've heard claims that suggest that less than 5% of the people in the United States regularly invest in their own self-improvement. If this is true then up to 95% of the people walking around in this country have not taken an adequate amount of time to take an honest look at themselves. If you want to create a new and improved watch then you had better understand what makes a watch tick. By understanding the current condition of an object we are better equipped to improve it. That is why builders survey land. They need to know the nuances of what they are building upon.

How aware are you of what makes you tick? What are your fears? What are your blocks? What are the core strengths that you have deep inside that will help you overcome anything? These are important questions to ask and be able to answer if you want to take your confidence to the next level.

Now I know that many men especially dislike looking at their emotional world. Some see emotional investigation and expression as wimpy or weak. What I would suggest to these people is that they are sacrificing a crucial component of developing a competitive edge in business and in life. When we understand ourselves well, what motivates us, what frightens us, what our strengths and challenges are, then we are much better able to adapt and make things happen. The confident person looks within and emphasizes strengths while adapting or correcting weaknesses. The less secure person deflects personal insight for fear of failure or threat to his ego. He misses the growth that can come from insight into his internal world.

THE ASSIGNMENT

One of the easiest and best methods for understanding your internal world is journaling. There is no one magic way to journal, but most methods simply require paper, a pen, and a few moments of reflection. During the next twenty-four hours keep a journal with you. Focus specifically on your feelings during this time. What frustrates you during your day? When do you feel your absolute best? What builds your confidence? In contrast, what shakes it? Who makes you feel good about yourself? Who annoys you and why? Remember that this is not just a journal of events in your day, but rather is a way to track your emotional responses to the events in your day. So every entry should have a feeling connected with it such as happiness, anger, hurt, joy, embarrassment, excitement, fear, love, or wonder.

While there are natural limits to how much you can learn about yourself in a twenty-four hour period of time I also trust that this will give you a taste for what you might discover if you were to journal on a regular basis. If you find great value in journaling then continue this as a daily or weekly practice to see what you may discover about your inner world of confidence.

BEING 100% RESPONSIBLE FOR HOW YOU FEEL

I was thinking of my patients, and how the worst moment for them was when they discovered they were masters of their own fate. It was not a matter of bad or good luck. When they could no longer blame fate, they were in despair.

—Anaïs Nin

THE RESEARCH: Confirming What We Already Believe

Hypothesis bias (also called confirmation bias) is a common tendency that most of us share. The theory states that once we form a hypothesis or an opinion about something we tend to look for evidence that supports our opinion and ignore evidence that refutes it. Therefore, if you form an opinion that your neighbor is a jerk, then you will tend to notice all the jerky things that he does. You are basically compiling evidence to make yourself feel righteous about your hypothesis. If this neighbor that you have labeled a jerk does something nice, like shoveling part of your sidewalk in the winter, you are more likely to assign some negative motive to his behavior. Possible interpretations could be "he must be wanting to borrow something" or "I bet he's just trying to get off the hook for mowing over my roses last summer." Hypothesis bias allows us to hold on to our opinions once we form them and is what makes it so difficult to change someone's mind once it is set.

Reference: Evans, Handley, Harper, & Johnson-Laird, 1999.

THE APPLICATION

What is your hypothesis about yourself as a human being? Do you see yourself as a capable, intelligent, and hardworking person, or do you think of yourself as a loser, or just average, or as an impostor? Whatever your hypothesis, you are likely to look for evidence to support it. So if you believe that you are average then you will focus and notice things that you do that show average abilities while missing the times when you are extraordinary. If you think of yourself as capable then you are more likely to notice capable things that you do and ignore or write off times when you are not as capable. This later tendency can help you in building even greater confidence. If I truly believe in myself then I will take note of my accomplishments and hard work. I will also learn from any moments when I do not do as well. The only time that believing we are capable does not serve us well is when we feel consciously capable, but subconsciously inferior. When this is the case people tend to not learn from mistakes because they can never admit that they make any! The secret is to take 100% responsibility for your actions, your feelings, and your belief in yourself.

Do you take 100% responsibility for how you feel about yourself? Do you take ownership for your level of confidence? Many people do not. In fact, we have lots of factors that we can blame for not reaching our peak level of confidence. "My parents criticized me growing up." "My boss is keeping me down." "My spouse doesn't support my dreams." Face it, finding someone to blame for our feelings or our "inability" to achieve our goals is pretty easy. Why is it so easy? Well basically, people will always let you down in some way. It is part of the human condition to fail. And I am the last person on this planet that would pretend like someone failing you does not hurt and sometimes hurt deeply. Yet why is it that people can go through nearly identical situations and some go on to commit crimes while others go on to wallow in mediocrity and still others go on to do incredible things? If our situation dictated our emotions and our success then we would not have this level of diversity in accomplishment.

Having spent years studying successful people, one of the factors that almost all of them have in common is that they take 100% accountability and responsibility for their feelings as well as their successes and failures. Many successful and confident people have been through horrible situations in childhood and young adulthood and yet I have never met a truly confident person who does not see their past as a crucial part of what has made them successful. Most of them take the attitude of "sure that happened to me, but I had a choice of how I was going to respond to it." In fact, many confident people almost make a subconscious vow that they will overcome their past. They certainly refuse to use their past as a form of excusing anything less than their best behavior.

Taking 100% accountability for your feelings and actions has many powerful impacts. The first is that you simply try harder. If you believe that failure would be your responsibility then you are going to work harder to avoid failure. If you believe that success is in your hands you will work more diligently to get there. A second benefit is that taking 100% accountability inspires those around you. I am often called into situations of conflict in corporations and one of the most difficult parts of my job is to get those in conflict to take 100% responsibility for their part in the communication. The most common response is a fear that "If I take that level of accountability then the other people involved will start blaming me even more." What actually happens is the opposite. My clients find that when they take ownership for their own emotions and actions, then the other workers involved soften their stances and start taking more ownership for their own feelings and behavior. One hundred percent ownership inspires others to interact with more humility rather than playing the blame game, which can escalate quickly and get quite ugly.

A third benefit of 100% accountability is peace of mind. People who lack confidence must blame others when something goes badly. To look at themselves is just too frightening. Have you ever met someone like this? They have an excuse for everything! In fact they can form elaborate excuses that are basically impenetrable. However, underneath their defensiveness is a wounded ego that lives in fear. The fear of exposure, the fear of being revealed as an impostor, and the fear of seeing their genuine self in the mirror. By taking 100% accountability you are basically saying, "It is OK that I am human," "I am still a valuable human being despite my flaws," and "Well, here's another learning experience" rather than being obsessed with the possibility of being a loser or failure. To be able to admit one's faults, be genuine in one's humanity, and hide nothing allows an incredible peace of mind and builds confidence to the next level.

THE ASSIGNMENT

What is your hypothesis about yourself? Use this assignment to become aware of this and/or shift this belief to the next level.

If you were to fully believe in yourself, what ten words would describe the best of who you think you are? Some examples are: intelligent, caring, capable, and tenacious. Write down ten adjectives that you genuinely feel are true about yourself at your best:

1. _____   6. _____

2. _____   7. _____

3. _____   8. _____

4. _____   9. _____

5. _____   10. _____

IMPACTING EMOTIONS WITH ALL OF YOUR SENSES

Only as high as I reach can I grow,
Only as far as I seek can I go,
Only as deep as I look can I see,
Only as much as I dream can I be.

—Karen Ravn

THE RESEARCH: THE IMPACT OF OUR SENSES

Author Alan Loy McGinnis states in *Confidence: How to Succeed at Being Yourself* that there are five crucial factors that create results from visualization. The five practices to use while visualizing are:

- Visualize in a regular time and place
- Picture whatever you visualize happening in the present
- Be realistic about what you visualize (although I would add, just barely)
- Visualize in the first person (rather than seeing yourself like a ghost floating above)
- Use all of your senses (not just what you see)

These five practices will help you create a visualization that hits on multiple levels.

Reference: McGinnis, 1987.

THE APPLICATION

Years ago, a couple I know were trying to sell their beach condominium and had walked several visitors through the condo, but had no offers yet. They had another couple coming and were anxious to sell, so I brainstormed with them some ways to pump up the attraction of the condo. We decided to create a multisensory experience. They did the usual of cleaning the condo, but then added a few extras. They also:

- Fired up the grill on the deck using mesquite charcoal
- Started cooking juicy premium hamburgers
- Made margaritas with umbrellas sticking out of them
- Had just enough people over to have a good conversation, but not make the condo seem crowded

So when the buyers arrived they were greeted to the smell of the grill, they could hear the fun conversation on the deck, they got to taste our perfectly cooked hamburgers, and they could sit down and feel the soft furniture while they visualized hosting their friends in this wonderful condo. They made an offer that day. We didn't sell a condo, we sold a multisensory experience!

When you think about it, the logic is irrefutable. Since we experience the world through multiple senses, why wouldn't we tap into these to change ourselves internally? Imagine watching a movie without the soundtrack. Imagine hearing the surround sound without seeing the picture. It just isn't nearly as powerful if you only involve one sense. Our senses are very closely tied together. Just try this visualization:

1. Imagine seeing the door of your refrigerator
2. Open the refrigerator and find a bright yellow lemon, noticing how saturated it is in color
3. Feel the coolness of the lemon in your hand and notice how plump and juicy it seems
4. In your mind, envision yourself using a small knife to cut open the lemon and listen to the knife hit the cutting board and the juice squirting out
5. Bring the lemon to your nose and smell the citrus
6. Now bring the lemon gently down to your mouth and take a big juicy bite

If you are like most people and really imagined all of these senses then you likely had increased salivation in your mouth. Amazing isn't it? There is no lemon and yet your body reacts as if you just bit one. This simple demonstration shows the power of our minds to impact our bodies.

Given that deep confidence can be highly emotional (rather than logical) in nature, the individual who wants to grow his or her confidence to an unusually strong level must associate confidence to the five senses. When I do confidence workshops for corporations, I like to walk the participants through their five senses to help bypass their conscious minds and impact their confidence on a more primal level. After getting the participants in a receptive mood I ask them five sets of questions. The first question is "What does confidence look like to you"? I want them to form a visualization of unbreakable confidence. The answers are quite varied. Here are a few I have heard recently:

- It is me hanging on the ledge of a huge mountain and pulling myself up with strength and ease
- It is the sun setting on the Mediterranean with a palette of colors that only God could paint with
- I see myself surrounded by my friends and family and knowing that nothing can break our love
- I visualize a fire burning bright and strong, resisting a downpour of rain because it refuses to be put out

At first, I have them take a few moments to really imagine what this looks like. I have them create nuances to their image and pull it up in their minds and hearts with vivid colors and details. After a few minutes of visualization I then pull out a sample of answers from the audience and watch with great joy, the faces and emotional responses as they share these beautiful and powerful images with each other. The next question is "What does confidence sound like?" Recent answers include:

- Beethoven's 7th symphony where the underlying rhythm is constant despite the introduction of new instruments and notes around it
- It sounds like my grandmother's voice
- Confidence is the sound of a small brook that gracefully flows under, over, and around rocks and other obstacles
- It sounds like thunderous applause after a job well done
- Confidence sounds like rock and roll, loud, strong and played without apology

Then we take a moment to try to hear it. I also encourage participants to find ways in their lives to surround themselves with these sounds. Next is smell, for which I hear things like:

- It is the sweetest smell you can imagine; like the freshest air that you can breathe in
- Success smells like fresh-baked bread
- Confidence is the smell of sweat after a hard workout that lets you know you pushed yourself hard
- It is definitely "Polo" cologne
- Success smells like a deep green forest after a cleansing rain

Next comes the sense of taste:

- Confidence is a fine cabernet sauvignon with a rich aftertaste lasting long after the first sip
- It tastes like that first sip of coffee out on my deck while the sun is coming up

- Confidence is the taste of hot cocoa that warms your entire body on a cold winter day
- It tastes like a perfectly cooked and seasoned steak right off of the grill
- Confidence tastes like chocolate, nothing else, it is definitely chocolate

Finally, we cover the sense of touch or texture:
- Confidence feels like the hand of God reaching down touching my face letting me know that everything will be OK
- It feels like a fur coat covering my entire body
- Confidence is crunchy
- It feels like a small sun burning hot and bright in the center of my chest
- Confidence is the feel of soft velvet that is smooth to the touch, but resistant to being torn

After we walk through these exercises the audience is invariably smiling and laughing or just sitting back in their chairs with a satisfied look on their faces. The experience of walking through the senses actually impacts their feelings of confidence at a deep and satisfying level. Now we are not just talking about feeling more optimistic and confident, we are experiencing the emotional centeredness of tapping into and growing our confidence even if just slightly, in that very moment.

THE ASSIGNMENT

Explore the power of your subconscious by tapping into all of your senses. Find a quiet spot in your office or home and put some deep thought and feeling into the following five questions. Then practice tapping into these senses in the days and weeks to come. In other words, when you want to shift your confidence then walk through all of your senses and see how it impacts your feelings of confidence.

1. What does confidence look like to you? What visual captures success and unbreakable self-esteem?

   _____

   _____

2. What does confidence sound like? What sound causes you to stand tall and feel unbeatable?

   _____

   _____

3. What does confidence smell like? What is the aroma of success?

   _____

   _____

4. What does confidence taste like? What is the flavor of success?

   _____

   _____

5. What does confidence feel like? What texture captures the spirit of confidence for you?

   _____

   _____

3.5

USING ART, MUSIC, AND MOVIES TO CHANGE YOUR LEVEL OF CONFIDENCE

If you hear a voice within you say
"you cannot paint," then by all means paint,
and that voice will be silenced.

—Vincent Van Gogh

THE RESEARCH: How Our Mood Impacts Our Confidence

The title of my doctoral dissertation was "The Effects of Mood State on Physiological Responding and the Utilization of Self-control Training." Basically it was a study asking the question "Does our mood impact our self-control?" The experiment had several steps, but the parts that are applicable to our current discussion are as follows:

1. Participants were given a task that required self-control and the ability to persist with a difficult task

2. Participants were randomly divided into one of three groups:
    - Those in group A were shown a stand-up comedy routine
    - Those in group B were shown a sad short film about a girl visiting her ailing grandmother
    - Those randomly assigned to group C simply waited for the next stage of the experiment

3. We assessed the mood of the participants

4. We tested the participants again with the task requiring self-control and persistence

5. We assessed how participants thought they did in the self-control task

What we found is that inducing a positive mood in someone can increase their self-control and tolerance for adversity. Interestingly, while a negative mood did not necessarily hurt their performance, it did impact their evaluation of their performance. In other words, the participants put in a negative mood thought they did worse than they actually did. According to self-efficacy theory it is likely that they would have actually performed worse if we had them do the self-control task again.

THE APPLICATION

The obvious application of my research is that mood can impact our self-assessment of performance. As stated in chapter 1.2, our self-assessment of our ability or self-efficacy has a strong effect on our actual performance. Therefore, it seems crucial that we guard our moods and emotions since they can dictate how we perceive ourselves and our abilities.

I have found that music, art, and movies are three simple ways to impact my emotions. What music do you listen to when you want to get pumped up for a presentation or meeting? I have a six CD changer in my car and you never know what you are going to find in it. From Christian rock to eighties pop to alternative music from the nineties, there are just certain songs that get my energy flowing and my confidence soaring. Or take a song like Louis Armstrong's "What a Wonderful World." I mean, here is a man who experienced great challenges and prejudices in his life and he could have easily written just songs of doom and gloom about the pain of life. However, he wrote this beautiful piece that never fails to remind me to appreciate what I have. Or how about the soundtrack to the movie *Braveheart*? That music gets me shouting "Freedom!" in my car every time (you'll have to see the movie to understand). This of course, amuses all of the other drivers, but at that moment I am so confident that I don't care!

Art has touched souls since the beginning of mankind. From the work of the masters to movie posters to inspirational photography, the visual nature of art impacts our emotions. I personally enjoy the works of Vincent Van Gogh and stand amazed at the beauty this troubled soul could create. I also marvel at the fact that he couldn't make a profitable income painting while he was alive and yet today his paintings sell for millions. What art moves you?

And then we have movies. I must confess to you that like my father before me, I am a huge movie buff. I have an in-home theatre and one of my favorite things to do is to watch a really good movie. Movies combine the power of sight and sound to make us cry or make us laugh (or sometimes both). When I am in a bad mood, I know which movies to put on to cheer me up (like the Holly Hunter classic *Living Out Loud*). When I am confused, I know what movies will center me again (like *My Dinner with Andre*, which people either adore or just don't get). When I am disconnected from my feelings, I know which movies will move me to tears (like *My Life* with Michael Keaton). And when I need to be inspired and charge up my confidence batteries, I know what films will do the job (have I mentioned *Braveheart* yet?). For years I have used movies to impact and direct my feelings. It is both effective and enjoyable and can shift my heart and my energy when all of my mental strategies fail me.

THE ASSIGNMENT

Build a list of works of art, music, and movies that impact your confidence. Expose yourself to one of these today. What type of music, art, and movies inspire you and build your confidence? Try to write at least three down for each category.

Music:

_____

_____

_____

Art:

_____

_____

_____

Movies:

_____

_____

_____

Want to share your ideas? We have created a section on our website www.advantagecoaching.com for readers to share movie, art, and music choices that impact them.

3.6

NEUROLINGUISTIC PROGRAMMING (NLP): A PROVEN METHOD TO IMPACT FEELINGS

We are all such a waste of our potential, like three-way lamps using one-way bulbs.

—Mignon McLaughlin

THE RESEARCH: NLP

Neurolinguistic programming (NLP) is a model and set of techniques that focus on how the interaction between the brain, the body, and language creates successful behavior. It was developed by UC Santa Cruz professor John Grinder and a graduate student named Richard Bandler in the mid-1970s, as well as formed from the work of famous therapists Fritz Perls, Virginia Satir, and master hypnotist Milton Erickson. "Neuro" relates to knowledge of the brain and how it works; "linguistic" refers to verbal and nonverbal communication and information processing; "programming" has to do with the thinking and behavioral blueprints we encounter. Taken together, neurolinguistic programming is the study of the structure of our personal or subjective experience.

In recent years NLP and has been made popular by motivational speakers including Anthony Robbins, who promotes these techniques heavily in his work. While the research on NLP is still in the infancy stage, practitioners offer dramatic claims of the effectiveness of these techniques. NLP has been used with phobias, weight control, sports performance, business success, and many other areas related to top performance or achievement. NLP is less of a theory than a collection of practical tools and approaches to change. Therefore, if a particular technique doesn't prove effective, a more effective one can be selected.

Reference: Grinder & Bandler, 1975.

THE APPLICATION

One of the things that I really love about NLP is that it is highly focused on practical techniques for impacting your emotions. It always amazes me how many people will pay for therapy when treatment consists only of talking about their feelings each week. Not that talking about your feelings is not helpful. Mind you, research shows that after a traumatic event such as an earthquake, divorce, or getting fired, one of the most important things to do to make sure that you heal from the event is to express your feelings. On the other extreme, it is surprising to me how little people are encouraged to deal with feelings in the workplace. "It is just business," we are supposed to tell ourselves, without letting our emotional lives enter in. Well, I have two words for you, "Good luck"! Try as you might, it is impossible to keep feelings out of the office. Even if feelings are not acknowledged or expressed they will motivate, impact, and, at times, sabotage your goals or effectiveness.

So in therapy I believe we often spend too much time talking about feelings (versus doing something about them) and in the workplace we try to create a fantasy world where feelings don't matter. The power of neurolinguistic programming is that it acknowledges feelings at a deep level, but has techniques focused on impacting these feelings and building them in a way that helps you meet your goals and become incredibly effective, and yes, confident.

I believe that the workforce that ceases being afraid of feelings and rather fully embraces them and works to create an emotional flow of success will be far more successful than their counterparts. Having and using the ability to impact your emotions can give you an incredible competitive advantage in an intensely competitive environment. So let go of the notion that cognitive or intellectual tactics are superior and get into yourself as a being of mind, body, and heart! Try it and watch the results!

THE ASSIGNMENT

Try this simple but powerful NLP-inspired technique. First come up with an image that represents low confidence for you. This should be a snapshot in your mind. It may be an image that involves you or it could be a different image (like one of your boss looking critical). The point is that it should be an image or mental picture of an event that currently has the power to drain your confidence. Then come up with a mental image that boosts your confidence. Form a mental picture that may or may not actually involve you, but has the power to energize your self-esteem and make your confidence soar. For example, one image I use is finishing a speech in front of one thousand people and getting a standing ovation. As a public speaker this image is very energizing for me. You might imagine landing a really big account or leading your team to incredible results or creating a life for your family that you always wanted. It doesn't matter what your image is, it just matters that your image is one that speaks to you. Come up with whatever mental snapshot builds your confidence. Once you have an idea of these then follow these steps:

1. Close your eyes and imagine the negative image that drains your confidence.
2. Now imagine depleting that image of all color; make the image completely black and white (this represents taking the emotion out of the image).
3. Then mentally move the image further and further away from you until it becomes a small gray dot.
4. Next, mentally recall the positive image that builds your confidence.

5. Energize yourself by imagining this positive image in full vivid color; have the image completely fill up your mind.
6. Now shrink the image down and bring back the negative image (keeping it dull and gray)
7. Now quickly shrink down the gray image and fill your mind with the full-color positive confidence image.
8. Repeat steps 6 and 7 several times.
9. Now stay with the confidence-building image and allow the negative one to disappear.
10. Finally, if your positive image is of yourself in some situation, see the situation from your own eyes (in other words become the person in the image rather than seeing yourself in the third person).

These ten simple steps can be completed in a few minutes' time and have the potential to shift your emotions and let go of any event draining your confidence. If you practice this technique you can call it up in any situation where your confidence is challenged and you need a quick recharge.

APPLYING YOUR FEELING STRATEGIES

Case Study

At twenty-seven, Simone had accomplished more than people twice her age. She was incredibly successful in the real estate business and was living a life that few of her peers could even imagine. She earned a hefty six-figure salary, traveled to foreign countries on a whim, spent freely, drove a sports car and had the world by the tail. Simone appeared to have confidence to spare. In fact, some people saw her as somewhat arrogant. However, she would just write these people off as jealous of her incredible success.

Then it happened. Without sharing the ugly details here suffice it to say that Simone overstepped her boundaries and got involved in some unethical dealings. At one point she realized that what she was doing was wrong and she decided to stop the behavior. However, she tried to cover up her "sins" and was eventually caught and turned in by one of her jealous peers. Up until this point she had felt invulnerable and no one was more surprised by her fall than she was. When a reporter for the local paper got wind of the story,

Simone even managed to make page two of the newspaper. Her license in danger of being revoked and her reputation sullied, Simone left the real estate business in shame.

Simone found my name on the Internet and called for an appointment. In our first meeting she shared her story with me in detail. She kept asking herself, "Why? I had everything going for me; why did I do this?" Coaching is often about "What do I need to do?" and "How do I do it?" but in this case it seemed very important to answer Simone's "why" question. I started the coaching process by having Simone journal her daily feelings and look for triggers to her emotions and reactions..

By our third meeting the "why" was apparent. Simone's journal helped her realize that part of her drive in life was to prove her father wrong. He had been a very critical man and would often tell Simone that she would never amount to much and should find a good man to take care of her. Simone had moved out of her house at seventeen and for the last decade had been working furiously to prove her father wrong. She had two drives that led her to get greedy and get involved in her unethical behavior:

1. She was subconsciously trying to get her father's approval and therefore needed to be even more successful and rich

2. She had internalized part of her father's voice and felt like she didn't deserve success (therefore unknowingly had to sabotage her success)

In other words, her hypothesis bias was made up of the competing beliefs that she had to be successful to be worthwhile and yet she didn't deserve to be successful in the long term. Simone's pattern is not uncommon. Each of us seems to have an internal limit to the level of success that we will allow ourselves. However, Simone had never (up to the point of coming in my office) taken the time and energy to look at herself and her emotions. She was too busy driving herself to success to look inside. However, not examining her drives and desires caught up with her.

At first, Simone wanted to completely blame her father for her failure. However, after an appropriate amount of venting and introspection she was able to move to 100% responsibility for her own emotions and actions. She realized reasons behind her actions, but was not going to use these reasons as excuses for her behavior. Through some coaching and encouragement Simone was able to accept her failure, make things right with those she had hurt, and eventually return to her business.

It was a challenging struggle and she had to use many of the emotional techniques mentioned earlier in this section. For example, she meditated daily using her five senses to rebuild her confidence. She used comedies, music, and photographs to encourage herself when she felt shamed and down. She became especially fond of movies such as *The Apostle* that showed the main character making terrible mistakes or facing huge adversity and coming back stronger. She also practiced the NLP technique of shrinking failure images and enlarging peaceful images that included grace for past mistakes. Fortunately, she approached her healing with the same level of determination she had approached her business success but without the self-sabotage.

Today she is doing well financially, but is also at peace with herself and no longer needs to prove herself to her father. She gets an incredible kick out of people mentioning how humble she is for someone at her level of success.

Don't take the same risk that Simone took. Take the time to understand your internal world and gain greater insight into your feelings and drive. Even if you are at the top of your game right now, try to discover what primal feelings might sabotage your future. Even if you do not have any past issues to conquer, use the emotional techniques to take yourself to the next level of confidence and success.

The Challenge

Review the feeling strategies presented in the five previous chapters. Which emotional strategy seems most helpful to you?
- Journaling to explore your inner world of confidence
- Hypothesis-testing what you truly feel about yourself
- Using all of your senses to expand your emotional confidence
- Using music, art, and movies to boost your confidence
- The NLP tactic involving color, distance and size to remove unwanted feelings

Your challenge (if you choose to accept it) is to take at least one of these techniques and make a commitment to how you will apply it on a regular basis in your life. Write your commitment to yourself here:

I commit to _____

_____

_____

I will do this every _____

_____

_____

BEHAVIORAL STRATEGIES:

ACTIONS THAT CREATE CONFIDENCE AND SUCCESS

GET READY TO ACT CONFIDENTLY

It Makes You Wonder

Even though they were both sixteen years old, the two boys could not have been more different. The first boy was shy, meek, and was a target for bullies at his school. His very presence seemed like a magnet for the football players who needed someone to humiliate that day. Even though he never said a word to them, they could just sense that he was someone who would be easy to humiliate. They would knock his books out of his hands in the halls and push him into the lockers whenever they passed. The boy's confidence was so low that he was always picked last for sports. No one wanted him to be on their team. His worst nightmare was when the coach would announce that it was dodgeball day. Humiliation came in frequent and strong dosages. He was depressed, withdrawn, and felt like he had very little to offer to the world. He hesitantly asked out one girl his junior year in high school but was a nervous wreck on the date because of his insecurity.

His counterpart was the complete opposite. On the summer following his junior year in high school he became a summer lifeguard at a church camp. This boy was picked first for almost everything. In fact, people loved to be around him. No one ever thought of bullying him because he never would have allowed it. He was active in all of the camp sports and would hit home runs in the baseball games. He lived with great joy and felt confident in what he had to offer the world. At the camp the counselors would often "date" for the week. If he was interested in someone, he would tell them directly because he was confident that they would also be interested. And if they weren't he could handle that just fine. He felt good about who he was and what others thought of him.

What you should know is that these boys were from the same family. They had the same genes, the same parenting, the same siblings, but could not have been more different. The other thing that is intriguing is that they are the same boy.

The Lesson

I have just described for you my junior year in high school compared to the summer of that same year. Because of the respect and expectations that came with being a lifeguard, I transformed from a shy, insecure "nerd" to a confident young man. As I acted more confident, I actually became more confident. The experience changed my life and taught me a valuable lesson about the choices we make and the impact those choices have on our lives.

Confidence and behavior are closely related. Most people would readily admit that you can tell a lot about the level of someone's confidence from his or her behavior. Sometimes you can even read a person's level of confidence from the way he stands, sits, and walks. So we can see how behavior stems from confidence. Yet is it possible that confidence can also grow from behavior? My level of confidence had nothing to do with why I became a lifeguard. I just wanted to hang out at the pool all summer! However, the action of becoming a lifeguard had an incredible impact on my confidence. Our choices and actions can either help our confidence grow or can diminish our confidence if ruled by fear or poor choices. In this section we will look at how changing your behavior can help you grow your confidence to the next level and bring greater success.

But first let's dispel another confidence myth.

Being a psychologist and executive coach I have had the privilege of working with CEOs, top executives, pastors, and other leaders. Let me tell you that NO ONE has it all together. Everyone makes mistakes on a regular basis. I don't care if you are Dr. Phil, Oprah, the president, or any other recognized leader, you are still a human being and your behavior will always be there to keep you humble. There are no gurus who have it all together.

This belief in gurus or in our own perfection is quite dangerous. When someone gets knocked off the pedestal, the fall is quite painful (for that person and those around the individual). The opposite harmful perspective is when we deny all the wonder and talent and beauty in each of us. We are human which means we are both talented and goofy, we can do magnificent things and we can be petty and vindictive. It is all a journey to tap into the part of God that lives in us and can create wonders in our life and for those around us. So while our actions will never be perfect, we can still work to minimize negative actions that could diminish our confidence and our success.

The Preview

The next six chapters will focus on action or behavior strategies for moving to the next level of confidence. With an action focus we will:

- Explore what gives you energy and what steals it away
- Learn a crucial element that must accompany your goals in order to be successful in moving your confidence to the next level
- Examine a technique that helps you face fears that could diminish your confidence in a step-by-step fashion
- Learn another technique for handling confidence-reducing fears that is harder, but faster, than other techniques
- Summarize all of these strategies and direct you to picking those action strategies that speak to you best and will aid you on your confidence journey

DEFUELERS
AND REFUELERS

It ain't what they call you, it's what you answer to.

—W.C. Fields

THE RESEARCH: Stress and Success

Stress is not just all in the head. Studies have shown that people who experience high stress are more likely to develop viruses and infectious diseases than people experiencing low stress. This and other research has supported the theory that stress can actually decrease our immune system and makes us more susceptible to physical exhaustion and mental illness. While some stressors are outside of our control to change, many others can be avoided or eliminated if we just take a look at what decreases our energy and what increases it. Face it: infectious diseases, exhaustion and mental illness in most cases do not bode well for success.

Reference: Cohen & Herbert, 1996.

THE APPLICATION

Often when I do a workshop on confidence or life balance I use an exercise that was shown to me from an excellent coach named Dr. Bob Rausch. The exercise involves having participants get into small groups of three to six and start making a list of the things that defuel them or take away their energy. Invariably these lists include such things as:

- Waiting in airports
- Bad news on the television
- Customers not returning phone calls
- Rainy days
- Angry people

What is usually very interesting about this activity is the number of items on this list that reflect things that we can't control. I can't control the weather, I can't control angry people and (as much as I wish I could) I can't control late airplanes. When we look at things that defuel or steal our energy many of them are things that are completely outside of our ability to change. There must be a lesson in this!

Why do we allow ourselves to get so bent out of shape concerning something we can't control? When you really think about it, this tendency makes no sense! The truth is that most of us like the illusion of being more powerful than we really are. We desperately work to scratch and claw and find any piece of power that we can. Kids are a great example of this. Psychologist Tom Phelan, the author of *1-2-3 Magic: Effective Discipline for Children 2–12*, once made a great point to me. He asked me why a child would misbehave even in the face of intense punishment. I came up with all sorts of theories, but when it came down to it, he had a great point about power. He said, "Think about it, a child has very little sense of power. You are bigger than them, you control the money, and in essence you can control most of their life. However, if that child can get you upset, then he feels a sense of power." This is why when disciplining children, you will be more effective to do it without emotion. One of the goals I have had with my own children is to try to help them find better ways to feel powerful than getting me upset. If I got upset when disciplining then I just reinforced their rebellion.

So from early on we want power. This tendency continues as we grow older. Often, all of our yelling at the customer service person because the plane is late is merely a subconscious way to feel a sense of power in a situation where we have little or none. A key to eliminating defuelers in your life is to move your focus away from things you can't control and learn to focus more on things you can control. In our list of defuelers I could shift my focus in a way that I felt recharged rather than drained and stressed.

- Waiting in airports—I could focus on getting some calls made or celebrate some time to myself where I don't have to accomplish anything
- Bad news on the television—I could turn the channel

- Customers not returning phone calls—I could view this as a challenge and focus on being creative
- Rainy days—I could find indoor activities that I enjoy
- Angry people—I could focus on my behavior and how I react to them rather than getting upset about their actions (or I could avoid them)

Gary DeMoss, a fellow trainer and speaker, uses the analogy of playing a tennis match. If you are in a tennis match and you smash the ball over the net to make an incredible shot then you will likely win the point. However, if your racquet goes over the net and hits it then you will automatically lose the point. To win the match you need to play well and make sure that you keep yourself and your racquet on the correct side of the net. If you continue to focus on things you can't control then your racquet is on the wrong side of the net and you will lose the match every time, even if you are the superior player! When we focus on things we can't control then we drain ourselves and create an incredible amount of stress in our lives. Confidence cannot thrive in that type of environment. Confidence grows and expands when we focus our thoughts, emotions, and actions on those things that we can impact and control.

THE ASSIGNMENT

Get a pad of sticky notes and a pen. Spend a few moments thinking about things that steal your energy. Write one draining thing per each sticky note. Keep writing these and tearing them off until you have exhausted your ideas on energy or confidence drainers. Then put your sticky notes up on the wall. Divide them into three categories:

- Things I can't impact or control
- Things I can impact, but can't control
- Things I can impact and control

Within each of these categories move your sticky notes around to prioritize which things exhaust your energy and confidence the most to which ones have less impact. You should now have a hierarchy of draining activities or people in each category.

Now pick one of your top three drainers in each of the categories. Today we will focus on building an action plan for the item that you can impact and control. Additional activities for the other categories can be found in the back of the book.

Things I can impact and control

Sometimes we are 100% responsible for the activity that is draining us. Maybe you have gotten into a habit of drinking too much when out to dinner or not getting enough sleep in the evenings. Your item in this category usually requires a choice to stop or change a bad habit. So for this item, what is your strategic plan to eliminate how you are allowing this to drain you? Write your action plan here:

_____

_____

_____

_____

_____

GOAL-SETTING

Confidence is the result of hours and days and weeks and years of constant work and dedication.

—Roger Staubach

THE RESEARCH: Goals Alone Are Not Enough

Research has shown that goal setting alone is not the best way to improve performance. One study compared the performance of four groups who received different combinations of goals and feedback. The four groups were:

1. A control group who did not receive goals or feedback
2. A group who just received goals
3. A group who just received feedback
4. A group who received both goals and feedback

The only group that showed a significant increase in effort as compared to the control group was the group that received both goals and feedback. While this sounds simplistic, my experience working with many companies is that very few collaborate with employees to create stretch goals and then also give frequent and specific feedback along the path to growth. For many companies, review time is a feared or hated event that simply becomes about compensation. This is unfortunate because companies and individuals are missing some great opportunities for growth. So if you want to change and grow, set goals and get constant feedback.

Reference: Bandura & Cervone, 1983.

THE APPLICATION

Are your goals big enough? Even if you have accomplished incredible things that have people around you singing your praises, are your goals big enough? When you really assess your talents, abilities, and drive are you honoring how you have been made and what you are able to do?

There is a parable in the Christian Bible that talks about a ruler who gave each of his servants a certain amount of money to take care of while he was gone. Ironically, certain translations of this text refer to the money as talents. One servant was given one talent, another two talents, and yet another five talents. Two of the servants invested the money wisely and when the ruler returned they were able to return to him his talents along with great interest. However, one servant was frightened of losing what the ruler gave him and therefore buried his share in the ground. When the ruler returned the servant came to him and said something along the lines of "See, I guarded what you gave me. It is all here!" In the parable, the ruler was furious. He had entrusted his servant with a talent and the servant merely protected it and never grew it.

The moral of the story is that we are supposed to use the talents that God gives us. In fact, it is our duty. To some He has given a little and to some He has given a lot, but the amount is not the issue. What we do with the talents is what is crucial. So how have you been blessed? Of what are you capable? When you look deep inside, have you set your sights high enough? Have you really allowed yourself to dream about the results, impact, relationship building, and quality that you can bring to the world? It's not just a good idea to do so, it is your solemn duty!

THE ASSIGNMENT

What is your "good enough" goal for this year? That one goal that may be tough to reach, but you are pretty sure that you will reach it. This is the goal that when you achieve it you will not be incredibly surprised, but you will feel a good level of satisfaction for achieving it. List that goal here. Try to make it as specific as possible and put a time frame on it. Also, attempt to make the goal measurable. How will you know for sure that you have achieved it? For example, "I want to lose ten pounds by June 1 of this year." Then make a list of the actions or behaviors necessary to achieve that goal.

"Good Enough" Goal:

_____

_____

Actions that will help me achieve my goal:

_____

_____

_____

Now, forget "good enough" and shoot for the moon. What is one goal that you are not positive that you will be able to reach this year, but you would be thrilled to meet? This is your ideal goal; that goal that is barely within the realm of possibility and would take using your talents, abilities and efforts at a maximum level. Really take some time to dream about this goal and then write it here. Or if you want to get really creative you can write it and draw it here in full bright colors (just a little trick to involve your subconscious). Then again create a list of the actions or behaviors necessary to achieve that goal.

Ideal Goal:

_____

_____

Actions that will help me achieve my goal:

_____

_____

_____

Mark on the following continuums your level of commitment for these two goals:

I am committed to achieving my "good enough" goal at the following level:

I am committed to achieving my "ideal" goal at the following level:

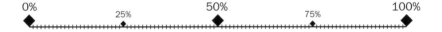

Now call up a friend who you trust will be excited about your goals and share them. Ask him or her to check in with you weekly or monthly to see how you are doing in using your talents and achieving these goals. Look for others who can give you feedback on your progress.

EASE INTO IT

You gain strength, courage, and confidence by every experience in which you really stop to look fear in the face. You must do the thing which you think you cannot do.

—Eleanor Roosevelt

THE RESEARCH: Reducing Fear

A tried and true method for decreasing fear is systematic desensitization. This tactic involves having the fearful person build a hierarchy of fearful events in order of the amount of fear the event creates. For example, if you are afraid of asking your boss for a raise you might build the following hierarchy from least feared to most:

1. Asking boss for a personal day off
2. Asking boss for more vacation time

3. Asking boss to set a meeting to discuss compensation
4. Asking boss for a cost of living increase
5. Asking boss for a 10% raise
6. Asking boss for 10% raise and bonus if you meet defined results

Most hierarchies are based on ten items and the individual is asked to imagine each of the events until he no longer feels the fear. Other methods such as relaxation training are often paired with this technique, which has proven to be very useful for anything from phobia of snakes to behaviors such as asking for a raise. The decrease in fear can be done mentally (by imagining the events) or it can be done by systematically exposing yourself to each event until you overcome the fear and are ready to go to the next level of feared behavior.

The relationship between fear and confidence is a strong one. However, confidence does not mean the absence of fear. I believe that confidence means that fear does not have control over what you do. Giving in to fear can have a very negative impact on your confidence. Reference: Wolpe, 1958.

THE APPLICATION

Fear of public speaking is often something that holds people back in their vocational success. Some research suggests that people are more afraid of public speaking than dying (although I once "died" on stage, thus combining these two big fears together—it wasn't pretty). So let's say that you are being considered for a big promotion, but part of what you need to do is build more of a public presence in the company. Your manager has suggested that you need to present before the bigwigs in the company to show your capabilities. You are not 100% confident that you can present in a way that would help you get that promotion.

If we were coaching and we had enough time then we could use systematic desensitization to help you overcome your fear of presenting (if we didn't have time then we would have to use the technique of flooding found in chapter 4.6). I would start by having you build a hierarchy of fears related to presenting. This list would be highly individualized, but could look something like this (going from the lowest threat to your confidence to the highest):

1. Presenting informally with those you manage
2. Presenting informally one-on-one with your boss
3. Presenting informally in a team meeting with your peers
4. Presenting formally with those you manage
5. Working up an icebreaker for a formal presentation
6. Preparing a formal presentation using PowerPoint
7. Presenting formally one-on-one with your boss
8. Presenting formally in a team meeting with your peers
9. Presenting informally for the CEO and executives in the company
10. Presenting formally for the CEO and executives of the company

We would then work through each of these systematically (either mentally or in practice) until you felt highly confident in your ability at that stage. If you were working with a coach then you might combine other factors such as filming your presentations for feed-back or relaxation skills; however, it can also be effective to practice each of these on your own and get feedback from peers and managers. The important thing (again, time permitting) would be to practice, practice, practice at each level until you were ready to advance confidently to the next level.

THE ASSIGNMENT

For the assignment in this chapter we are going to do an exercise similar to one we did two chapters ago. Once again, get a pad of sticky notes and a pen. Now brainstorm all of the things that you have been avoiding that have an impact on your confidence. Then do the following:

- Write one feared action or activity on each sticky note. These can be work-related or home-related. Keep writing these and tearing them off until you have run out of things that you have been avoiding.
- Start putting them in order in terms of their impact on your confidence. For example, you might be avoiding asking your spouse to change a behavior at home and might also be avoiding calling a former customer who is upset with you. Which of these has more of a negative impact on your confidence? Order them accordingly.
- Now take off any sticky notes that represent things that you really should avoid because you objectively know that facing them would be more destructive than helpful (but make sure you are honest with yourself about this).

• You should now be left with a few items that, due to your avoidance, are keeping your confidence from being at the highest level possible.

Now, pick one activity from the list you've made, and form a plan of attack by answering the questions below about it:

1. What do I need to do to overcome my fear of this action?

_____

_____

2. How will it benefit me to face this fear?

_____

_____

3. How will it hurt me to avoid this fear?

_____

_____

4. What action do I need to take with this (break it down into a smaller initial step if needed)?

_____

_____

5. When will I do it?

_____

_____

YOUR BEST PERFORMANCE

Courage comes from wanting to do it well.
Security comes from knowing you can do it well.
Confidence comes from having done it well.

— Author unknown

THE RESEARCH: The Illusion of Helplessness

It is natural for all animals and humans to avoid pain. However, research on learned helplessness has found that you can actually teach animals to falsely believe that pain is inescapable and thus cause them to accept their circumstances and experience pain when they could avoid it. The experiments involved restraining dogs while they received an electric shock. When the restraints were taken off the dogs could have avoided shock (like the unrestrained dogs) by jumping over a barrier. However, the dogs did not jump over the barrier and instead endured the shock unnecessarily. Because of their previous helplessness they formed the illusion of having no control over their fate.

While this is a simple (and some might add, cruel) experiment, are we really so different than these dogs? Who do you know that is staying in a bad situation that she could get out of if she would only see the possibilities? History proves that opportunities will come from challenges. Those who give up control and become helpless will miss significant possibilities and opportunities. Optimistic and confident people do not believe that helplessness will last and merely bide their time to seize the opportunity.

Reference: Seligman, 1975.

THE APPLICATION

When we believe that our actions are meaningless, we will give up on pursuing our goals. Unfortunately, most goals that are worth attaining require us to go through multiple failures and trial and error in order to succeed. If you look back over your past you will realize that most of your best performances came from tenacity, learning from mistakes, and the willingness to experience failure before you experience success.

Some people feel as though their actions will not make a difference in their life. This can often be related to childhood challenges and feelings of helplessness. For example, one client of mine experienced a reoccurring nightmare of doing an important presentation before his peers and he could not get anything to work. His computer would reboot on him spontaneously, his PowerPoint presentation was missing slides, and he could never find the notes to his talk. In the dream his peers would walk out of the room disgusted at his lack of ability and professionalism.

You don't have to be a psychologist to see that this reoccurring nightmare was about his sense of rejection and powerlessness. These perceptions dated back to a tough childhood and growing up in a single-parent home (desperately wanting his parents to reconcile, but having no power to make it happen). Despite his success, he still feared feeling powerless again. These feelings shaped him over his life and impacted both his greatest successes and his greatest failures. If he could not conquer his deep feelings of helplessness, his success would be impacted negatively. Fortunately, in time he learned to come to grips with his personal power and, to my knowledge, never had the nightmare again.

What is your belief in your personal power? Do you believe that your actions will eventually lead to success or do you become overly discouraged by temporary failures? To meet your maximum level of success, you must believe that your actions have value and will eventually lead you to your goals.

Three chapters ago I spoke about the illusion of power and how we need to embrace those things that we can't control instead of fighting them. This is but half of the picture. The other half is that we have to break the illusion of helplessness also! We are neither as powerful nor as helpless as many people believe. In most situations there is some element that you can impact. To believe in complete powerlessness creates a victim mentality and erodes confidence.

Part of being incredibly confident is to always find something to impact no matter how difficult the situation. Learned helplessness creates doubt and hesitancy which can be very dangerous during difficult times. Confidence creates hope! If I try hard enough, long enough and wisely enough I will find some way out of any situation. It is like the incredible movie *The Shawshank Redemption* where the Tim Robbins character spent decades chipping away at his cell wall in order to escape his unfair imprisonment. Part of the suspense of this movie is wondering if he was going to give up and kill himself or if he would find a way to keep going.

In our society, things have come quickly and easily to some people. Our attention spans are decreasing and we are upset if the microwave takes a full three minutes to complete our meal. We see what others have and we want it, but we want it quickly and without the dedication that the goal will require. This has to change in our society in order for us to recapture what has made us great. We must find joy and excitement in challenge. We must celebrate the character that we build by facing tough tasks that seem impossible and yet we find some way to conquer. We must never give up too easily because of the illusion that if it doesn't come quickly then it won't come. We must never believe that we are helpless.

THE ASSIGNMENT

One surefire way to demolish any doubts or feelings of helplessness is to remember and emotionally re-experience times when we felt great impact and power. The act of mentally recreating these events can give us a great boost in confidence, especially in challenging times. Remembering our most successful times can fuel us and also help us remember what has made us successful. In the following exercise, I will encourage you to bring back to your consciousness the experience of a great success. Think of a time when you worked long and hard to reach a goal and did succeed. Recreate an event such as a sports victory, a business breakthrough, a big sale, a personal victory (such as losing weight or quitting smoking), a time you were able to really help someone, or any other time in your life that you felt great about meeting a goal. Look for practical insights that you can apply to move to the next level by considering the following questions.

Remember back to your best performance ever and answer the following questions concerning that experience:

How did you prepare for the event?

_____

_____

What habits helped you to be successful?

_____

_____

What can you learn from that experience to help you thrive in the current environment?

_____

_____

Bring this information to mind the next time that you face a difficult task that will require you to be your confident best!

FACE IT

> *While one person hesitates because he feels inferior, the other is busy making mistakes and becoming superior.*
>
> —Henry C. Link

THE RESEARCH: Just Do It

Several chapters ago I discussed a way to decrease your fears slowly and methodically. Well, if you are like me, you would rather take the quick and more difficult approach which can be more immediately painful, but also very quick and effective. A flooding technique takes the thing that you're avoiding and, well, basically puts it in your face. This technique has been shown to drastically reduce unrealistic fears. So, as opposed to systematic desensitization when I used the example of slowly working up to asking your boss for a raise, flooding would immediately have you either visualize asking for a raise until your fear subsided, or actually ask for a raise and work your way through it.

By exposing yourself to something you fear and staring at it long enough it eventually loses its power over you and can no longer impact your confidence.

Reference: Ost, 1989.

THE APPLICATION

What are you afraid of doing? What actions are you avoiding that might be impacting your confidence? Few things can destroy our confidence as much as avoidant behavior. However, the great thing about flooding our fears is that if you keep exposing yourself to any irrational fear then your fear will eventually diminish and go away. Avoidance builds fear; exposure decreases it (as long as the fear is irrational and you stay exposed to it long enough). Salespeople who were initially afraid of cold calling can vouch for the relief that simply comes through practice. It is hard to stay afraid of cold calling after your 300th call and you see that nothing bad happens to you from people saying no (and in fact some great things happen to you when they say yes).

Flooding is an appropriate technique to use when you need to build your confidence quickly. For example, let's say that you are asked to give a public presentation at your company's annual meeting and you have never spoken before such a large audience before. Your flooding technique might be to find as many opportunities to speak before people prior to that event. You would speak for your son's fifth grade class on career day, provide business insights for a large chamber of commerce function, and volunteer to make the announcements before your congregation. Basically, you would dive into every speaking situation you can find so that by the time your spoke at your company function, your confidence would be dramatically increased.

We must face what we fear. Whether it be at work or home, avoidance of fear simply decreases your overall level of confidence. Every time you avoid something you fear (especially if the fear is irrational) there is a little voice in your head that says "You can't handle it" and then you prove the voice right by running away. Now, I'm not saying that you should put yourself in the face of true danger, I am just saying that when you avoid something, make sure it is for a good reason and does not decrease your confidence. Nothing should have that power over you. Nothing.

I have seen so much unnecessary pain come when clients avoid actions that will help them. Here are several examples of confidence breaking activities reported by past clients:

- The client that turned down a promotion she really wanted because it would involve some public speaking
- The person who would not turn in expense reports because he was afraid his boss would be upset due to their lateness
- The salesperson who could talk a good game, but still feared rejection and thus would avoid closing the sale
- The manager who would not confront one of her peers who often degraded her in team meetings
- The coach who would not raise her rates to market standards out of fear of losing her clients (yet complained about not making enough money)

- The husband that would always overpromise and under-deliver to his wife when it came to promises about traveling less
- The entrepreneur who was running out of funding as he kept procrastinating his marketing because he could never perfect his brochure
- The client who would never ask for a raise, but was constantly furious at her boss for not giving her what she "deserved"
- The small business owner who avoided any form of negotiation with his vendors and rather would take whatever price they offered

I have a rule that I encourage my clients to embrace. That rule is that in the absence of any logical reason to avoid a behavior, you should immediately do any feared action that you need or want to take. If I am afraid of it, then I do it. As long as there is no true danger and there is a good reason for facing something, I encourage people not to procrastinate even for a brief period of time. Because every day you procrastinate builds your fear and slowly erodes your confidence. Now sometimes we need to hold off due to preparation factors or needing to analyze a situation fully. However, that type of hesitation is driven by wisdom, not by fear. If irrational fear drives it, then little good can come from avoidance.

THE ASSIGNMENT

What is one task, activity, or action that you should be doing, but have been avoiding due to an irrational fear? List it here and answer the following questions:

I've been avoiding _____

_____

What is your worst fear of what would happen if you took this action? _____

_____

How is your avoidance impacting your life? _____

_____

_____

What positives would come from facing it? _____

_____

_____

Given your answers, what should you do: continue to avoid it? Or do it?

If your answer is to do it, then set a date here: _____

APPLYING YOUR ACTION STRATEGIES

Case Study

Judy realized that she was capable of more, but she also was capable of far more than she realized. Judy was assigned to me as a coachee by her boss. She was hesitant about the embarrassment of others finding out that she had a coach until I explained to her that organizations only use coaches for highly talented, high potential people in the organization. I helped her change her view of coaching from a punishment to a perk. We were working together because her boss knew she was more talented than what she was showing. One of Judy's main blocks was that she was overly concerned about what others thought about her. This level of concern held her back from confronting subordinates on poor performance, tardiness, interactions with other departments, and other problem behaviors. It also made her too risk-averse for the position that she held (she was too afraid of what others would think if she failed).

When we first started talking I asked Judy what was the main goal for her coaching. She said, "I don't want to care what others think of me." We discussed the benefits and costs of that goal and I encouraged Judy to set that as her ideal goal. I also encouraged her to set a "good enough goal" given her first goal was such a radical shift. Her good enough goal was, "I can still care what people think, but I will not allow that to control me or stop me from doing the right thing." I thought this was a more realistic goal and one that we could definitely meet.

Part of building Judy's confidence for change was to look at her best performances from the past. As we pulled these up from memory, I could see Judy change physically. She sat up a little taller, she had more energy and she actually appeared to be somewhat feisty. As we analyzed her best performances we noticed a couple of trends:

- She took a risk
- She had to confront different opinions
- She had to rally the team to performance

Bringing Judy back to that moment, mentally, increased her motivation and built her self-efficacy. She knew she could do this. As we looked at the issue Judy started realizing how ludicrous it was for her to try to control what people thought of her. She had an "aha" moment when she realized that paradoxically, trying to control what others thought of her was actually responsible for her boss thinking poorly about this area of her performance. The plan had backfired! It was now time to focus on those things she could control, like making the best business decision she could and confronting poor performance respectfully.

The biggest breakthrough for Judy came in the form of embar-rassment. We had gone back and forth on which of the two fear-busting techniques to use (flooding or hierarchies). Eventually Judy decided to go the more painful, but faster route. Her assignment was to do something embarrassing before our next session. It had to be something that would truly be hard for her to do. Well sure enough, she came through. Her embarrassing activity was to "acci-dentally" knock a glass of water all over the conference table during a meeting with her boss and several of her peers. While this was not an activity I probably would have chosen, what she found was that the sky did not fall and the world did not end when she "made this mistake." After several assignments of embarrassing herself, she felt she had made a breakthrough and was building freedom from the concern. Not surprisingly, she performed much better on her job and ended up with a raise and a promotion despite her infrequent "clumsy behavior."

By exposing herself to the embarrassment that she feared, she actually overcame her fear and became a more optimistic, confident and productive leader in her company. For Judy, facing the fear of others thinking poorly of her changed her view of herself and oddly enough actually made her more respected, more liked and more valuable to the company.

The Challenge

Review the action strategies presented in the five previous chapters. Which behavior oriented tactic or tactics seem most helpful to you?

- Focusing your actions on those things that you can control
- Setting good enough and ideal goals for yourself

- Tackling your fear hierarchy to overcome blocks to confidence
- Tapping into a previous top performance to build your confidence
- Doing something embarrassing in order to break out any confidence inhibitors

Take at least one of these techniques and make a commitment to how you will apply it on a regular basis in your life. Write your commitment to yourself here:

I commit to _____

_____

_____

I will do this every _____

_____

_____

SECTION 5

RELATIONAL FACTORS:

DEVELOPING A COMMUNITY THAT RECHARGES RATHER THAN DRAINS

GET READY FOR A COMMUNITY THAT BUILDS YOUR CONFIDENCE

It Makes You Wonder

I'd like to share with you two horror stories in public speaking. One has a terrible ending and the other has a happy ending. Let's start with the one that went badly.

My very first corporate speaking opportunity left much to be desired. A good friend of mine was traveling around the country doing a very successful "boot camp" for one of the major financial services firms. His part of the workshop was receiving perfect ratings from participants, but he had a sales psychologist doing other parts that were met with a mixed reception. Therefore, he asked me if I would like to develop and institute a program to train the financial advisors concerning the psychology of success. I was thrilled to have the opportunity.

I decided to work up a talk on cognitive strategies to overcome any fears they might have in dealing with prospects and clients. I interviewed financial advisors in order to get specific examples of common fears and felt confident as my friend and I started heading off to the West Coast to do this presentation. My excitement turned to hesitation as I sat through my friend's initial part of the presentation. The group to whom we were presenting were some of the top financial advisors in this firm and to be honest, they were being downright rude. They were chatting with each other during his talk, taking phone calls on their cell phones, and a couple of them were even practicing their golf swings back by the coffee station. Despite my concerns, I used some good self-talk strategies on myself to boost my confidence to present before this disruptive group.

As I started my presentation I could tell that the group was restless and I tried to increase my energy to capture their attention. My presentation came to a crashing halt when one "gentleman" stood up in the crowd and defiantly confronted me saying, "What the hell makes you think that anything you have to say applies to me?" The room got deathly silent as his verbal gauntlet was thrown. What in the world do you do in this kind of situation?

My first response was to try to convince him about the applicability of my examples, but he just argued that I had no concept of his world. Then I switched tactics to encourage him not to think about the particular examples, but to learn the techniques from the examples to deal with any different fears that he had. At this point he bluntly informed me that he had no fears and that my techniques were stupid. If dead silence can get even more still, then that is how quiet the room was at that point. In desperation, I turned to the rest of the group and asked, "Well, is anyone here afraid of anything?" After thirty seconds of silence (that felt like thirty minutes) an older gentleman sitting by the defiant participant raised his hand. His simple comment was, "Uh, I'm kind of afraid sitting next to this guy." Thankfully, his humor broke the tension in the room and I was able to get back to my presentation. However, being a rookie in public speaking at this point in my career, I let myself get too rattled by the experience and ended my presentation an hour early.

At dinner that evening I was drowning in my failure and feeling terrible about myself. My confidence was shot and I swore I would never do corporate speaking again and especially never in financial services. At this point my friend informed me of something he had just discovered. The discovery was that unlike previous sessions which were voluntary, these highly successful financial advisors had been forced by threat to be there. Add to this the fact that the boot camp took away their entire weekend and just to add insult to injury, they were forced to pay $1,000.00 to attend. In other words, we walked into a hostile audience whose hostility was aimed at us despite the fact that we were oblivious to what had happened. This information allowed me to recover my flailing self-esteem and today I do corporate speaking and coaching for a living and have a large part of my clientele in the financial services industry.

Flash forward to the late 1990s. I had the great opportunity to speak before an international crowd on the topic of coaching. There were only about 100 individuals in the workshop, but they were some of the best and brightest managers from around the world.

They were invited for this weeklong workshop on leadership, of which I had one session. By this time, I was much more seasoned as a speaker and again was confident despite the cultural barriers that might be present.

As I was confidently sharing my views on the philosophy and skill sets of coaching, a woman from France interrupted me. With defiance reminiscent of my previous story she challenged what I was saying. "This coaching thing makes no sense, I am not here to babysit my people. If I tell them to do something they should just do it," she announced. Fortunately, by this time I had learned how to handle disruptive individuals and simply looked at the woman and said, "You know, you are absolutely right! If a manager is babysitting her people then something is horribly wrong with her approach. I think we all have seen managers who coddle and micromanage their people and the results are devastating for everyone. So thank you for clarifying that point because coaching is absolutely not about babysitting, but rather about empowering people." At this point she leaned back in her chair satisfied that I had heard her wisdom and I could then go on without interruption. However it was clear to me that there were significant cultural issues that could separate some of us in that room if handled poorly.

The Lesson

I share the first story of my "failure" to show how our individual confidence is not independent from what is going on with the people around us. Interactions with others have a huge impact on how we feel about ourselves. I share the second story both to show a better way of handling confidence challenges in the relationships around you, but also to start the discussion of differences in how cultures can view the same issue or situation. These cultural differences also exist in how different countries look at self-worth and confidence.

Psychology by Bernstein, Penner, Clarke-Steward, and Roy (2003) was an invaluable resource for leading me to much of the general research presented in this book. In one very interesting section, the authors review cultural differences in self-worth. They note how individualistic cultures such as the United States, Great Britain, and Switzerland promote the idea of self-worth as independent of others. They review research indicating that many individuals in North America and Europe focus on a development of personality that is unique and based on a sense of high self-worth. In fact, they quote one study (Markus & Kitayama, 1991) that showed a startling statistic. According to the study, 60% of U.S. students felt they were in the top 10% of their peers on a variety of positive attributes. Clearly the U.S. culture is very focused on self-enhancement and the need to stand out of the crowd in order to feel good about yourself.

In contrast, countries such as Japan, China, and Brazil promote a more collective orientation. In these countries people are taught to see themselves more as parts of a bigger system who need to blend in and not stand out in case they diminish someone else by their boldness. In these countries worth comes more from others' approval and living at peace with those around you.

It is senseless to argue which way is the right way. Obviously, both types of cultures have captured some important elements of self-confidence. Without the individualistic focus of the U.S. culture many great opportunities and advances would have been lost in this world. In contrast, the need to stand out and be different or superior has much potential for actually diminishing our ability to be interdependent on others. Often a community is much more powerful than any individual.

I believe that to focus all of our confidence strategies on the individual would be a mistake and it is one that many books of this type make. The previous three sections have been more focused on the individual. However, this section on community, and the one to follow on spirituality, look at the individual within the context of the world and community in which he lives. Unbreakable confidence cannot be a completely individualistic endeavor. You and I need others around us, and sometimes, just sometimes, they desperately need us also.

The Preview

In the following six chapters we will focus on community or relationship strategies for building your confidence. With this relationship focus we will:

- Identify people in your life that drain your confidence (even if you don't realize it)
- Learn how to increase your support network
- Examine how conflict impacts your confidence
- Explore the great value of feedback and how it helps address confidence challenges and blind spots
- Look at the roles of forgiveness and giving back to your community in upgrading your confidence (and the confidence of those around you)
- Move to applying the most effective community confidence builders

IDENTIFYING
THE DRAINERS

Other people's opinion of you does not have to become your reality.

—Les Brown

THE RESEARCH: How Others Impact Us

Take a group of women who are good at math and divide them into two groups. Inform the first group that men usually do better than women on a math test that they were about to take and show them information that supports this. Take the other group and give them no information and guess what? When the women expected that men would do better than them, they performed worse than the men. When they were not told that they were lesser, they scored equally to the men. Another obvious result is that the women who held their natural expectations did better than the women whose expectations were manipulated. This finding is called the stereotype threat effect and should scare all of us to some degree.

What are the people around you telling you about your abilities and capabilities? How are the people around you impacting your energy and your confidence?

Reference: Spencer, Steele, & Quinn, 1997.

THE APPLICATION

Mary was an extremely busy executive who had little time to spend with her family. She traveled often and was feeling a great amount of guilt over the lack of time she had been spending with her children. One way of making it up to her children was their annual trip to the amusement park. She would take them for the entire day, reluctantly leaving her cell phone behind, and do nothing but focus on the children having a great time on the rides.

The day was about half over and Mary was not in the best of moods. The lines for the rides had been ridiculously long and it was one of the hottest days in the summer. She was starting to lose her patience with some of the inefficiencies of the park and her children could tell that mom was getting in one of her moods. As they arrived to their favorite roller coaster Mary and her children were informed by the sixteen-year-old park worker that the ride was closed and they were not allowed to wait in line for it to open.

Mary actually liked it when the rides were temporarily broken down because everyone would jump out of line. Soon the ride would reopen and then she and her family could get on quickly. Therefore, she was annoyed that the young woman told her that she could not wait. Therefore, she informed the worker that she and her children were going to wait in line until the ride reopened. The young woman hesitantly told Mary that she was not allowed to wait and should go on to another ride. That was enough to set Mary off. She got in the sixteen-year-old's face and started yelling at her. The young woman turned bright red and looked like she was going to cry. "I paid a lot of money to come into this park and no kid is going to tell me what I can and can't do!" Mary screamed. She went on berating the employee to no end waving her arms and bringing much attention to herself. Her children were mortified and begged her to go to the next ride. After a few more verbal punches, Mary threw up her hands in disgust and stormed away with her children. She turned briefly to see the sixteen-year-old tearful and shaking from the encounter.

That night Mary was telling her husband about this incident, citing how inefficiently the park was being run and how she was thinking about sending a scathing letter to the management. It was then she heard the news report. She listened to the news anchor in horror as he reported that a person died on that particular roller coaster that day. She had been eating candy or chewing gum and had suffocated on the ride. The tearful and shaken face of the sixteen-year-old working flashed into Mary's mind. She then realized that this young woman had been dealing with the knowledge that someone had just died on the roller coaster and was trying to keep people away from the ride for that reason. Mary felt ashamed of her behavior and went to bed quietly, although she did not fall asleep for a very long time.

We must be careful of the assumptions that we make and we must guard how we treat others. That poor sixteen-year-old was likely traumatized by what was going on already and she did not need to be attacked for simply doing her job. It often amazes me how frequently we give ourselves permission to verbally berate someone in customer service or other environments when it isn't even their fault. Mary was quite embarrassed when she saw the news. Is Mary a lovely person who was just having a bad day or is she a person who feels free to spew anger over others in her path? Sometimes it is hard to tell. However, how often do we allow negative people in our lives? And what kind of impact does that have on us? We must identify and guard ourselves against people full of negative energy. If not, our confidence will suffer.

THE ASSIGNMENT

Perform an informal assessment of your community. Answer the following series of questions and make a decision concerning people who drain you.

1. Who are you in a relationship with who brings you down and steals your energy?

   _____

   _____

2. What actions do they do that specifically erode your confidence?

_____

_____

_____

3. How will you deal with them differently in order to guard your confidence? Be creative here and if possible, try to come up with approaches that can repair the relationship vs. just run from it (although there are times to drop a "friendship" and move on).

_____

_____

_____

4. Are you draining anyone around you? If so, what will you do about it?

_____

_____

_____

5.3

SURROUNDING YOURSELF WITH SUPPORT

Don't let people drive you crazy when you know it's in walking distance.

—Author unknown

THE RESEARCH: People Who Need People

Studies have shown that a significant part of our self-concept is our social identity. Our social identity is related to our beliefs concerning groups with which we affiliate. When you ask someone to describe himself you may get an answer focused on personal characteristics such as "I am a nice person" or "I am good listener." Other times, people will answer the same question within their social identity such as "I am a Chicago Cubs fan" or "I am a Catholic." Our social identity allows us to feel part of something bigger than ourselves and can be very powerful. Just think of the last time your team (in whatever sport) went up against another team. The camaraderie is amazing and all other differences seem irrelevant at that moment. Even when meeting someone new we just feel more comfortable if they belong to some group to which we belong ("Wow, you are from Chicago too—cool!").

Reference: Troop & Wright, 2001.

THE APPLICATION

The next time you are in a crowded area such as an airport or a mall, try a little observation experiment. Guess the main visual difference between people who are walking by themselves vs. people who are with others or talking with someone on a cell phone. The answer: people alone do not smile. Really, it is true for about nine out of ten people. Nine out of ten people walking alone do not smile. Oh, every now and then you get a sole man or woman smiling, but it is not often. In fact, one week I was waiting for an appointment at a coffee shop in New York staring out of the huge glass window when I turned to the woman next to me and said, "Hey, have you ever noticed that people walking by themselves do not smile?" She didn't believe me and started staring out to prove me wrong. But as she watched New Yorkers quickly walking by our window, sure enough my hypothesis was correct...for just a few minutes. All of the sudden she belted out,

"Aha! Look. There is a guy by himself and he is laughing and grinning ear to ear." Of course, I was disappointed in her observation until something became apparent to me. "Look again," I said, "That guy is obviously hallucinating." Sure enough, the man was having a fun conversation with his imaginary friend so my theory stood up to the test!

What is the point of this story? Basically, we need each other. We need people around us. Something in us yearns for connection. Therefore, it is crucial to surround ourselves with people who build us up. People who love us enough to challenge us when we are wrong and yet also be sensitive enough to ensure us of their love even in these times. A good friend with a genuine word of praise can do wonders for our confidence. A friend who can "speak the truth in love" can help us see areas of growth without threat and with the safety net that a good friendship provides.

We are fortunate to live in a neighborhood with a lot of kids, so my three boys have lots of community. I remember the first year we lived here my son had made friends with three other boys, Ryan, Tyler, and Pat. As kids would do, they had conflicts pop up that they had to work through. I remember one day sitting down with them and explaining the concept of "having each others' back." I don't know if that talk made an impact, but what I do know is that despite each having a different personality and each pursuing different things as they have gotten older, they do seem to truly support each other. Oh, they will "talk trash" to each other and jockey for the position of power, but I believe that if any bully tried to push one of them around, that the others would be there for him in a second. There is great protection when surrounding yourself with the right community.

What kind of community do you have in your home and in your work? Do family members, peers, managers, subordinates, and others in your life "have your back"? One thing that I have found surprising and somewhat sad in my coaching is the number of executives who do not have any really good friends. Oh, they have plenty of acquaintances and people at work who they like, but many of them have trouble naming a truly loyal friend who would never let them down. Why is this? Does our need for this type of support really change as we get older or do we just get too busy to nurture these types of relationships? Let's forget work for a second and just talk about home. Does your family have one another's backs? How many couples do you see who are constantly tearing each other down? How many couples do you know that publicly and enthusiastically build each other up and try to boost each other's confidence? Not many, I'd imagine.

Does it have to be this way or could it be different? What could it do for you to be surrounded by people that believe in and bring out the very best in you? What would happen to your confidence if you could try new and unpredictable things because you had a safety net of support behind you? And how could you impact those around you if you gave them this same gift? To surround yourself with support is not just a pipe dream. For the person who wants to live with confidence, it is a necessity.

THE ASSIGNMENT

1. Write down the name of one person who adores you that you would like to spend more time with.

   _____

   Now, pick up the phone today and schedule a time to get together. Talk with this person about getting together on a more regular basis.

2. Write down the name of one person who is great at "speaking the truth" to you "with love." It has to be someone who's got your back, but also cares enough to help you see yourself clearly.

   _____

   Call him or her today and show appreciation for this form of care.

3. If you have no one who plays this role in your life, how might you go about creating this type of friendship?

   _____

   _____

4. Name one person in your life to whom you would like to show greater support. How will you go about showing this person that you care about and believe in him or her?

   _____

   _____

DEALING WITH CONFLICT

I'm going to be more assertive...
if that's OK with you.

—Author unknown

THE RESEARCH: Conflict and Contact

One form of conflict is a result of prejudice and stereotypes (which are just extremes of our tendency to lock on to and exaggerate the importance of differences). Research suggests that as we spend more time with people who are different than us, our stereotypes and prejudices diminish. This is called the contact hypothesis. Not surprisingly, contact alone is not always helpful, but rather several other conditions must be met. One important condition was that people must get to know and understand each other as individuals in order to change the negative perceptions. However, in the midst of conflict, working to understand the other person is often just the opposite of what we feel like doing.

Reference: Pettigrew & Tropp, 2000.

THE APPLICATION

I was once driving cross-country with a friend of mine who decided that he was going to open up to me about his sex life (one of the blessings and curses of being a psychologist). Without prompting, he went on for at least forty-five minutes about the intimate details of his relationship with his wife. He discussed what he liked, what she liked, what he disliked, what she disliked, etc., in far more detail than I plan to write about in this book. So after his forty-five minute intimacy monologue he switched to another subject—money. As he started to talk about his dissatisfaction with his income, I casually asked, "Well, how much do you make?" His reply back to me was, "Tim, that's pretty personal."

What is the moral of the story? People are different. Perhaps because of my conservative upbringing I am not one to talk about details of my sex life. However, I have always been open about money. I was open when I was poor and I've been open when I've done well. To me, money is not personal. To my friend, the opposite was true. So who is right? Well, obviously, neither one of us. We just think differently. Those differences are part of what make our world beautiful and diverse and creative and fun. Those differences are also what cause wars and fighting and pain and rejection.

What is the impact of conflict on your confidence? When the conflict is in a win-lose arena (like a sports game) then our confidence can be impacted by our status as the winner or loser. However, in relationships, win-lose scenarios are not what we should be trying to create. In fact, scenarios in which all parties can "win" are more likely to build personal confidence along with a community that supports you. I have found that the easiest way to build loyalty with others is to help them get what they want in life. If you help others reach their goals most will naturally want to help you reach yours.

The topic of conflict is huge and if this is a major area of your life I suggest that you pick up my previous book, *The Coward's Guide to Conflict: Empowering Solutions for Those Who Would Rather Run Than Fight* (shameless plug). However, for this chapter let's focus on one technique to decrease conflict in your life. That technique is simply asking questions.

When I do workshops I always try to involve the audience as much as possible. One exercise I do comes from improvisational comedy. It is called the question game and in this game you are only allowed to ask questions. Once you make a statement to the other person you are "buzzed" out and a teammate comes in to take your place (like an intellect's version of tag team wrestling). On the surface this sounds like a simple game, but the truth is that most people do not last for more than two questions their first time out. We have been trained since early kindergarten on to answer questions instead of ask them. This training backfires on us in relationships.

Most people are slow to show understanding and quick to show an opinion. Think about it in your own life: how often do you feel that someone takes the time to ask you enough questions to fully understand your perspective before sharing her own opinion? Most of us would answer this question, "Not often enough." Of course, the flip side of this question is crucial also. How often do you ask enough questions of the other person to demonstrate your willingness and desire to fully understand his stance before sharing your opinion? If we are honest with ourselves, we will also answer this question with "Not often enough." The interesting thing is that you may think you understand the other person's stance when you don't. I recently had a friend furious at me for something I said. The only problem was, I never said it! He completely misinterpreted something I had said, when in fact, I was saying the opposite of what made him mad. Once he understood me, he was embarrassed by getting so upset about a misperception.

On other occasions we may be very accurate in our perception of what someone is saying and will start sharing our opinion back only to have him restate his position as though we never heard it. This is likely a sign that, although you understood what he said, he doesn't realize that you understand. This probably occurred because you didn't take the time to reflect or ask enough questions to "show" him that you heard him. When people don't think you've heard them, they will keep repeating their stance until they are sure that they are heard.

So, while this may seem like an unusual approach to self-confidence, I am encouraging you to support others and show them that you have heard them. Ask enough questions to show your interest and desire to really understand their perspectives. You will build your confidence two ways:

- By proving to yourself that you are centered enough in your own opinion that you are not threatened by allowing someone else to share her perspective
- By building the relationship and encouraging loyalty in other people

In the end, the more confident you are, the less defensive you will be and the more you will be able to ask questions vs. give answers to others.

THE ASSIGNMENT

Think of someone with whom you have conflict. Put yourself in his or her shoes. How might you show this person that you understand his or her perspective (even if you don't necessarily agree with it, you can still show that you get it). Write down three questions that you could ask this person to show a desire to understand his or her perspective:

1. _____

   _____

2. _____

   _____

3. _____

   _____

In what kind of spirit do you need to ask these questions? In other words, if you ask these sarcastically or mechanically, then this approach is likely to fail. Therefore, what emotions do you want to show while asking these questions?

1. _____
   _____

2. _____
   _____

3. _____
   _____

After filling out the above, make a decision about approaching this individual and trying to resolve the conflict.

ASK FOR FEEDBACK

You're never as good as everyone tells you when you win, and you're never as bad as they say when you lose.

—Lou Holtz and John Heisler

THE RESEARCH: Our View of Ourselves

We all form opinions about ourselves. Sometimes those opinions are very favorable and sometimes those opinions can be quite harsh. But how do we go about forming these views about ourselves? Well, if we have facts that are presented to us on a regular basis about our behaviors, habits, and tendencies, then we will often form our self-perceptions based on these. However, in the absence of objective evidence or proof, we turn to two different sources to judge ourselves. These sources are:

- How we were in the past
- How we are compared to others

Therefore, as I form my opinion about how I am doing, I will look at my past behaviors, accomplishments, and viewpoints. If I am doing better in these areas than I was doing in the past then I form a positive opinion about myself. I will also look at the behaviors, accomplishments, and viewpoints of others. Obviously, if I perceive that I am doing better than others then I will form a positive evaluation of myself. If I view that I am doing worse than others then I will form a negative self-evaluations.

Interestingly, we have many options to choose from. I had one client in financial services making $450,000 a year who considered himself a failure because he'd made slightly more the year before and was also constantly comparing himself to a select group of others in his field who made more money. If he had chosen to compare his financial success to the average income of his peers then he would have felt like a huge success. Our frame of reference is our choice and has great consequences to our confidence.

References: Wilson & Ross, 2000; Oyserman, 2001.

THE APPLICATION

Our view of ourselves is quite tainted. In the example of my client above, many of you will find it ludicrous that he felt like a financial failure. His frame of reference was tainted. This is why it is so important to get feedback and other perspectives from people around us.

Sometimes their perceptions can reveal flaws in our own viewpoints and also help us see things about ourselves to which we are blind. However, you must choose these feedback relationships wisely.

When it comes down to it, there are two types of people on this planet: those who will tell you when you have a piece of spinach in your teeth and those who won't. Oh, there are many justifications for not telling people that they have spinach in their teeth, or toilet paper on their shoes, or (heaven forbid) something hanging out of their nose, but the primary reason is that we don't want to embarrass them or even more so, ourselves. However, which is really more caring? I don't know about you, but if I have toilet paper hanging from my shoe, I hope that someone would care enough to tell me. Now, toilet paper on the shoe is pretty concrete, but I would also want someone to tell me something about my personality, habits, or behaviors that may be obvious to everyone around me, but to which I may be blind. I mentioned this earlier using a driving analogy, but want to emphasize it again here.

For example, I had a client who was an executive in the medical industry who was completely oblivious to the fact that he almost always started his responses to colleagues with the word "no." Even when he agreed with his coworker, for some reason he would start his response with this little two-letter word. For example, if a peer said, "I think that we need to respond quickly to this department because they are known to procrastinate," my client would respond, "No, you're right; we need to get back to them immediately." I watched this occur in a team meeting that I was facilitating and pointed out the behavior. His peers said, "Yes, he always does that, and it irritates the heck out of us. We wonder if he is trying to take the idea for himself." My client on the other hand was completely taken by surprise. He had never received feedback about his automatic use of the word "no" and had absolutely no idea that he had that habit. Once he realized it he started to laugh and asked his peers to point it out to him whenever he said "no" in order to help him break the habit.

Now, saying "no" at the beginning of your responses may seem like a little thing, but the important point is that it was completely hidden from him. Once I pointed it out and his coworkers validated the point, my client was able to make a conscious decision and try to change this habit. To build our abilities and our confidence we must be able to see ourselves clearly. We each have habits and behaviors that could keep us from reaching our potential. A lack of confidence means that we are threatened when people point out these hidden areas. The truly confident person will ask for feedback from others in order to develop and grow. Only insecure people are frightened of their own imperfections. You can tell a lot about a person's confidence by the way he or she responds to feedback. Defensiveness is often a sign of lower confidence.

I am often pulled in to corporations to work with highly talented performers who have difficulties working well with others. After forming a bond around goals and starting the development process, a common assignment I have for them is to form a list of people from whom to get regular feedback about their progress. Openness to this feedback serves two purposes:

- The added accountability of the assignment helps the individual change his behavior more thoroughly and quickly
- The humility of asking others for assistance impacts the community around him to become one more dedicated to his growth than his downfall

Of course, you want to choose your sources of feedback well. They must be individuals who will share the feedback directly, but with the same level of respect that they would want from someone giving feedback to them.

THE ASSIGNMENT

Write down the names of three people from whom you would like feedback.

1. _____

2. _____

3. _____

What type of feedback would you like (circle as many as apply):

- Feedback concerning possible areas of growth for me related to personal habits or common behaviors
- Feedback around a particular behavior (list it below)

_____

- Feedback on strengths and gifts that I have
- Feedback on how I relate to others

Consider approaching one or all three individuals concerning your desire for feedback.

FORGIVING AND GIVING

Forgiveness to the injured doth belong, but they ne'er pardon who have done the wrong.

—John Dryden

THE RESEARCH: How We Judge Others

There are several tendencies that have been studied in psychology that are important to understand in order to understand how we judge others. There are three I would like to share with you.

The fundamental attribution error: We tend to judge others' behaviors as reflecting something internal about them or their character rather than look at situational factors that influenced their actions.

The actor-observer bias: We tend to attribute our own behavior to situational or external factors (so if someone else does something bad it is because he is a bad person; if I do something bad it is because I had a bad day at work).

Hindsight bias: People say that hindsight is 20/20. They don't know how right they are. An interesting finding is that both positive and negative outcomes look more likely to have occurred when looking at them in hindsight. It is a scientific phenomenon that in hindsight all things look more predictable.

Therefore, when we make a mistake we tend to blame forces outside of us, but when someone else does wrong we tend to make judgments about her as a person. Then with hindsight bias we can judge her behavior as even more stupid and thus form a pretty harsh opinion of this other person. These findings are just part of why giving grace and forgiving others is not only important, but will have implications for our development as a confident and whole person. Reference: Gilbert & Malone, 1995.

THE APPLICATION

According to the *APA Monitor* online (volume 30; #7), Martin Seligman taught a seminar at the University of Pennsylvania in 1998 on positive psychology. One of the assignments involved students doing both pleasurable activities (such as going to a movie) as well as giving activities (such as helping a nephew with homework).

Interestingly, they reported that the effect of pleasurable activities was short-lived in comparison to the effect of giving activities. Acts of kindness that tapped into some skill set of the students and were spontaneous in nature had a much more lasting positive impact on the rest of the student's day. The lesson? Acts of kindness and giving make us happier and more centered. Therefore, it is not much of a leap to believe that giving can increase our success and confidence.

Forgiveness is an act of giving. Forgiveness can be costly because you are basically releasing someone from a debt that they owe you. True forgiveness can only occur when someone does not deserve to be pardoned. If they deserve it then forgiveness is not even necessary. But what do forgiveness and confidence have in common? Well, quite a bit, actually. The insecure person has a great deal of difficulty with forgiving someone who has injured her. The lack of forgiveness acts as a protective shield to keep further harm from occurring. Now, some people confuse forgiveness with saying that the offensive behavior was OK. Nothing could be further from the truth. If the "offensive" behavior were OK then there would be no need for forgiveness! We only need to forgive things that were truly harmful or offensive. And of course, forgiveness is a gift to be given only to those who are sorry and will cease their offensive behavior. Forgiveness is not permission for someone to continue to hurt you.

What you will find is that the willingness and ability to forgive actually increases your confidence. To truly let go of a harm that someone has done to you and is sorry about impacts your spirit because you are going beyond the desire to keep things "fair." To focus on fairness means you have to hurt the person back, and sometimes the main way to hurt him is to hold on to the hurt that he did to you. To refuse to be fair, but rather to forgive, is good for the soul and good for your concept of yourself. Lack of forgiveness tends to be self-focused. Forgiveness steps beyond your personal world and connects to something bigger (more on that in the spiritual section). Our confidence always grows when we refuse to react to others and take the high road.

Yet it isn't enough to simply live at peace with others, we must also find ways to give back to the world if we hope to actualize our potential. I believe that deep down most of us want to be decent people. And a natural part of wanting to be a good person is the idea of giving something back to the world. There are few things more pleasurable than giving to someone who really appreciates it. When we become self-centered then we are missing out on a great and easy way to not only grow our confidence, but also impact the confidence of others. Sometimes that gift can be monetary or some item of value. Sometimes it is a gift of our time. Other times we can give the gift of mentoring or coaching someone else. For example, my confidence has grown over the last couple decades from my work with helping others grow their confidence. I have gotten the benefit of learning from many clients even when I was in the role of teacher. I have gotten the sweet satisfaction of seeing others blossom into their potential. And I have gotten the great benefit of gratitude from others. Few things taste as sweet to me.

If you have read this far, then you have learned quite a bit about confidence. Perhaps it is time to start sharing your learning and experience with others.

THE ASSIGNMENT

The forgive assignment:

Call, see, or write someone who wants your forgiveness, but is unsure that you have forgiven him or her. Let this person know that you will no longer hold his or her actions against him and that you are forgiving him or her completely. If you need forgiveness from this person in return, do not be afraid to ask for it. If this step is too soon for you then make a commitment to work to let go of the offense so that both of you can be freed up from this previous pain.

The give assignment:

Do a "give back to the world" activity today. Here are some possible actions:

- Send money to your local church or charity
- Write a letter of encouragement for someone who is hurting
- Spend time with someone who has few friends
- Call that relative who would love to hear from you, but you call rarely
- Smile at someone passing you on the street
- Do something special for your family that is outside of the ordinary
- Compliment a complete stranger (such as a waitress or customer service individual)
- Go to the unemployment office and hand a complete stranger an encouraging book with a fifty dollar bill as the page marker (I know one person who did this with a Bible and $1,000, but walked out before the person opened it in order to do it anonymously)

- Tell your significant other what attracts you about him or her both physically and spiritually
- Do an act of service for a neighbor (wash his car, shovel his walkway, etc.)
- Write your own here.

_____

_____

In the end it doesn't really matter what you do. What matters is that giving back to the world is part of your weekly, if not daily, routine. You and your confidence will grow from this great activity.

APPLYING YOUR COMMUNITY STRATEGIES

Case Study

Austin was the CEO of a midsize company. He employed 150 people in his office and had an external sales force of almost eight hundred. His was a true "rags to riches" success story. He had always been a confident man and was a true inspiration to those around him. I met him the year that he wanted to grow his company to thirty million in revenue. However, he was blocked and for the first time in years he felt insecure about his ability to be the CEO of a company of that size.

Austin had nothing growing up. He grew up in the worst areas of Chicago and fought every obstacle that tried to block his success. Community was extremely important to him. I heard many stories of him helping others, serving the community, and showing great care for his family and workers. Despite his appearance of confidence, he had great difficulty saying "no" to people (including requests for loans that many people never attempted to pay back). He shared how he had some extremely negative friends who always wanted to do activities with him and that he even had a trip coming up to go mountain climbing with one of them that he wished he had never agreed to. Austin could not name a single friend in his life who gave him energy. He was the "perfect" friend to others, but he had not built a recharging community for himself. Of course he was afraid to grow to a thirty million dollar company! It would just mean that more people would need him!

As we problem-solved ways to free up more of his energy, delegate tasks, put boundaries in place, and build more support, he continuously shot down every idea. Finally, I stopped our session and looked at him straight in the eyes and said, "Austin, I have a feeling that you made some sort of a vow to yourself as a child about not letting others down. You made a vow that you would never abandon those who needed you. Am I correct about this?" After several minutes of intense silence, Austin looked up with eyes more like a hurt young man than a confident CEO and slowly said, "I told myself that I would never be like my father."

It turns out that Austin's father left his family in horrible financial straits and moved away without even telling them where he had gone. At that time, Austin became the "man of the house" and basically felt the need to take care of his family. He became the supporter, rather than remaining the supported, at too early an age, and it was an identity he would carry into adulthood. That identity served him well in many ways. It was part of his drive to be so successful.

It was part of his drive that helped him aid so many people. However, to go to the next level and to grow more confident, Austin needed to transform this drive.

So we reviewed some of the ways to help recharge him:
- Setting proper boundaries for requests for loans and other types of help
- Confronting negative people in his life
- Limiting trips and get-togethers with people who would not change their negative ways
- Finding a good friend or two who recharged him

Despite his fear of being like his father, once we revealed what was going on subconsciously and used a couple of focusing techniques, Austin was able to see that he could still be a caring, responsible, and community-minded man and at the same time protect his own strength and energy. In fact, he soon became convinced that he would be able to help more people if he protected his energy. He was no longer afraid of growing his company, because he had boundaries to protect his time and life. Therefore, once the block was gone the company began to grow again.

There was only one question left: what to do about his feelings toward his father? Given the good man that Austin was, his lack of forgiveness bothered him and, therefore, was on his mind. When we talked about this Austin realized that the main block to forgiving his dad was that he felt forgiveness meant saying his father's behavior was OK. What he eventually realized in our discussions is that forgiveness means "What you did was horrible, but I am letting it go and will not hold it over you; I am giving you grace." In time he forgave his father and is no longer haunted by the bitterness that lack of forgiveness puts in our souls.

Austin's company grew to thirty million and beyond. He is not afraid of more growth, he has a great community around him that has his back, and he continues to impact the world with strength, compassion and confidence.

The Challenge

Are relationships impacting your level of growth? Have you surrounded yourself with the right people? Are you giving back what you need to be giving back to others? Do you live with joy and grace or bitterness and lack of forgiveness? You don't have to be a doormat to live with compassion and you don't have to be a CEO to make a difference in this world.

Review the community strategies presented in the five previous chapters. Which relationship tactic or tactics seem most helpful to you?

- Assessing your relationships for their impact on your confidence
- Building support by pursuing those who recharge you
- Dealing with conflict to eliminate drains to your confidence
- Asking for feedback to face areas for growth
- Forgiving and giving to transcend to your next level of confidence

Take at least one of these techniques and make a commitment to how you will apply it on a regular basis in your life. Write your commitment to yourself here:

I commit to _____

_____

_____

I will do this every _____

_____

_____

SPIRITUAL

CENTEREDNESS:

DISCOVERING UNBREAKABLE CONFIDENCE BY LIVING YOUR PURPOSE AND MISSION

GET READY TO LIVE A CONFIDENT LIFE

It Makes You Wonder

I was relaxing on the beach with my wife when I heard the call for help. I looked around and there was a woman desperately screaming. As I looked out in the water I could see a young boy on a raft who had been pulled out into the ocean by the undertow. I yelled to my wife to get help and then I jumped in and started swimming for the boy. The waves were rough and the ocean was unforgiving that day. At the same time a young and athletic lifeguard heard the cry and started swimming out to the boy also. As we got out there it was all I could do to keep from being pulled out further into the ocean. The lifeguard started swimming the boy in, but it was not an easy task given the force of the undertow. As I started to swim back I noticed that we had another problem. The mother had impulsively come out into the deep with us, but was obviously exhausted and now in trouble herself. The lifeguard was now far ahead of me and I knew that it was up to me to get the woman to shore safely. The only problem was that I was exhausted myself. Getting back to safety seemed to take forever. For every two strokes forward the undertow would pull us back one. I alternated between actually carrying the woman back and having her swim herself and simply coaching her back to the shore. At one point I wasn't sure that we were going to make it. She was crying and saying that she had "nothing left" and wanted to give up. I refused to accept her doubts (even though I had the same doubts). Several times she was pulled under and I had to grab her hand as I kicked furiously to keep from being pulled back myself. I had never experienced a battle with nature like that and hope I never have to fight that kind of power again. Eventually, with a grateful mother in my arms, I felt sand beneath my feet. With a quick prayer of thanks I fell to the beach as we eventually made it back to shore.

The Lesson

I had never been afraid of the ocean up until that point. In fact, given that I was trained and worked as a lifeguard in my younger days, I didn't think twice before jumping into the ocean to go get the boy. My confidence was actually cockiness. I felt more powerful than anything the ocean could throw at me. My foolishness could have cost me my life. The ocean was far more powerful than I was and it was only through luck and grace that I made it safely (with a passenger in tow) to the shore. I learned a healthy respect for the ocean that day. And I slept for sixteen hours that night to recover.

No matter how confident we are, no matter how successful we become, no matter how powerful we feel, there is something bigger than us. To develop to our full level of confidence we must tap into that which is larger than we are. We have to embrace and flow with the limitless power that is beyond anything to which we could ever aspire. This section will deal with building confidence through spirituality.

The Preview

I make no apology in that I am a Christian and that I believe that life is a process of trying to submit to the will of God for our lives (I only apologize that my behavior often fails to match what I would ideally like it to be, which is why I'm thankful for grace). I also recognize that different people of different faiths or no faith will be reading this book. Therefore, for the purpose of this book (except for a few select points), I will be referring to spiritual in the broadest sense of the word and I believe that you can benefit from this section regardless of your religious affiliation. I only ask that you approach it with an open mind (as I try to do also).

In the following six chapters we will focus on the core of confidence and that is your spirit. With a spiritual focus we will:

- Explore your vocational calling (because when you are in the wrong career your confidence can be crushed)
- Examine the concept of moving from success to significance
- Uncover and address any integrity challenges or internal tension between what you believe and how you are acting
- Talk about the role of grace and connection to God and how both can greatly impact your confidence
- Build a personal mission statement that can help build unshakable confidence

- Summarize all of the spiritual approaches and concepts and move to an action plan on building your confidence by building your spirit

DETERMINING YOUR VOCATIONAL CALLING

> *You have brains in your head.*
> *You have feet in your shoes.*
> *You can steer yourself in any*
> *direction you choose.*

—Dr. Seuss

THE RESEARCH: What Creates Job Satisfaction?

Ask employers what causes employee satisfaction and most of them say the same thing—money. However, research shows that money is not enough to make someone happy in their job. Instead, satisfaction seems to be linked more to the following factors:

- Level of participation in decisions
- Being able to problem-solve
- Utilizing multiple skills
- A sense of responsibility
- Public recognition

Too many people stay in a job that, at best, drains them and, at worst, chips away at their souls.

Reference: Rosen, 1991.

THE APPLICATION

Randy was struggling with his confidence. He thought that he was going through a midlife crisis, because he was starting to question himself in ways that he had never questioned before. He came to me saying that he had been extremely successful in his career, except for within the last year: now his new boss was considering letting him go if he didn't kick up his performance. He reported that his confidence was shot and he had never felt less successful than he did at that moment.

About one year prior, Randy's company had merged with a larger company and things had gone downhill since that point. Randy was aware that some of this tension came from a shift in his reporting structure. He and his previous boss had gotten along very well. As long as Randy produced, his previous boss was "hands off" and Randy always produced. However, Randy's new boss was much more "hands on" and, in fact, some would describe his behavior as micromanaging. Randy felt like he had worked too long and too hard to have someone "baby-sit" him and was pretty resentful of the constant interference from his new boss. I had Randy do the Career Projection Exercise (which will be your assignment for this chapter) to get a sense of his wants, drives, and motivations in a career.

Randy discovered the following factors were important to him in his career:

- An entrepreneurial environment
- Opportunity for advancement
- Independence and freedom from control
- Opportunity to manage a team
- Travel opportunities
- High order problem-solving tasks

As we walked through the list, he realized that he used to have all of these needs met with his previous position. When the merger occurred his duties shifted to focus more on individual performance versus leading a team. He saw less opportunity for advancement. The newly merged company had representatives in places he used to travel (so less travel). And most importantly, the culture of the new company, as well as the personality of his new boss, favored more of a hierarchical structure instead of an entrepreneurial environment.

I had seen this situation many times. Mergers and acquisitions seem constant these days and unfortunately, merging the computer systems gets much more attention than merging the people. Forward-thinking companies are aware of the impact of different corporate cultures and use companies like mine to help people cope with the transition. Randy's transition was never dealt with except for threats of being fired if he didn't adapt more quickly. So armed with this insight Randy had three main options:

1. Look for another position

2. Work within the company to either change his position or see if it could be adapted to fulfill some of his needs

3. Accept his new position for what it was

When someone has vocational desires, wants, and motivations as strong as Randy's, I have rarely seen that third option work. Randy decided to give notice and look for another job. He found a position that better matched the things that drove him and, not surprisingly, his confidence came back full force.

None of us are immune to our environment and if you are in a job that does not play to your strengths and desires then your confidence will be impacted to some degree. However, when you are in "the zone," working in a job that flows with your gifts and desires, it is hard for anything to come between you and maximum confidence. Are you in the zone?

THE ASSIGNMENT

The purpose of the Career Projection Exercise (CPE) is to help you determine what you want in a job or career. Use the following instructions with the chart that follows.

1. Write your name in the box indicated.

2. For persons one through five, write the names of five people you know whose careers you are familiar with.

3. Now work through the chart, comparing each person's profession to all others' professions. Look for key differences and similarities in their career duties and functions. For example, for the first box, a difference might be that you may have a job that requires being around people while person 1 sits in a cubicle and works by herself. A similarity might be that you both work for small companies. For the next pairing a difference might be that person 2 has a job that involves selling a product while you sell a service. A similarity might be that you both manage people. Try to find one difference and one similarity for each of the career pairings; write the differences and similarities in the spaces provided.

Each box should contain unique job characteristics. This exercise will work best if you do not repeat characteristics but instead find a distinct difference and similarity within each job pairing.

Career Projection Exercise

List the names of the people here:				
Person 1	Person 2	Person 3	Person 4	Person 5

Me	& Person 1
Different	
Same	

Person 1	& Person 2
Different	
Same	

Person 2	& Person 4
Different	
Same	

Me	& Person 2
Different	
Same	

Person 1	& Person 3
Different	
Same	

Person 2	& Person 5
Different	
Same	

Me	& Person 3
Different	
Same	

Person 1	& Person 4
Different	
Same	

Person 3	& Person 4
Different	
Same	

Me	& Person 4
Different	
Same	

Person 1	& Person 5
Different	
Same	

Person 3	& Person 5
Different	
Same	

Me	& Person 5
Different	
Same	

Person 2	& Person 3
Different	
Same	

Person 4	& Person 5
Different	
Same	

Now that you've got the chart filled out, complete the following steps:

4. Look through the chart and circle the qualities and functions most interesting or fulfilling to you.

5. By circling these qualities, you've identified the job characteristics most important to you. Now prioritize these circled qualities to indicate what's most important to you in a job. Add to the list any other job characteristics that you consider critical.

Career Priorities

1. _____

2. _____

3. _____

4. _____

5. _____

6. _____

7. _____

8. _____

9. _____

10. _____

What you have created above is a template that you can apply to your current or potential job and career to help determine how fulfilled you will be with that position. Ask yourself these additional questions:
- How might you incorporate these values or functions into your current position?
- Is there a different occupation or business that would better incorporate values and functions that are of the highest priority to you?

FROM SUCCESS TO SIGNIFICANCE

Abraham Lincoln did not go to Gettysburg having commissioned a poll to find out what would sell in Gettysburg. There were no people with percentages for him, cautioning him about this group or that group or what they found in exit polls a year earlier. When will we have the courage of Lincoln?

—Robert Coles

THE RESEARCH: Why Success Isn't Enough

Erik Erikson identified eight stages of human development. Of particular interest is the middle age state of "generativity versus stagnation." In this stage adults either find some type of activity or work to impact the world or become inactive and self-focused. Many individuals face a midlife crisis or reevaluation to look at what they have done in their lives and what they want to do to leave a mark on this planet. Success tends to be an individualistic and self-centered activity. At this stage of life, many people turn from "Where have I been successful?" to "How can I create something of significance?"

Reference: Erikson, 1968.

THE APPLICATION

At twelve years old you have the world by the tail. Most boys and girls still feel innocent and fairly invulnerable when it comes to facing the world. However, this illusion was quickly broken for me. My mother woke me and said that we had to leave our house. This was 1972 and we lived in the town of Wilkes-Barre, Pennsylvania. The weather had been rough for days and we were informed that the town might be flooded. The radio was on and I could hear the announcer suggesting that we put our television sets and other valuables on top of our kitchen counters and tables in order to protect them from the flood. Of course, I was most concerned about my comic book collection and my mother told me that they would take care of it. My parents loaded us in the car and we drove off hoping for the best. Our hopes were turned to disappointment as the next day my father took a rowboat over the top of our home; he saw only the chimney sticking out.

In 1972 my family and I lost most of the "things" that we had accumulated in life up until that point. Interestingly, I think less of what we lost and more of what happened afterwards. We were in a local mall, homeless and not sure where to turn when a man came up to us and asked us if we were flood victims. As he heard our story he offered that my family of six could stay in his home until we could get back on our feet. Some acts of human kindness are beyond what a simple "thank you" can communicate. This was one of those moments. Yet a child doesn't know this. It wasn't until a few years ago that my brother and I returned to Wilkes-Barre. One of the first things that Ken and I did was try to find this person who was so kind to us to thank him as adults. Sadly, he had passed away some time before we got back there. Thankfully, however, his and his family's act of kindness far outlived his mortal life.

We lost every "thing" that we had, but the loss of the worldly belongings was overshadowed by the gift of another human being caring enough to open up his house to us in a time of desperation. Success brings stuff, significance impacts lives.

To transcend to a greater level of true confidence you must learn to move from success to significance. It is common for individuals in their mid-forties to make this realization. Many of us have met a lot of our goals by that time in life and while we are happy that we met the goals, we also realize that there must be more to life than simply making money and buying things. For some, this results in a midlife crisis; for the optimistic and confident individual, this is a wonderful time to recreate yourself for the second half of life. When we have impact and significance we have something that no one can take away. A flood can take away a television set, a comic book collection, and all of your furniture. A flood has cannot remove an act of human kindness or the impact that you can have on helping someone in a bad situation.

What kind of mark do you want to leave on this planet? What will be your significance for living in this world? When you have passed away and are just dust, what do you want others to say at your funeral? How do you want to be remembered? For me, I would hate to think that I would be remembered mainly for how much money I made or how much stuff I had. I would rather be remembered as someone who truly cared for people, and tried despite his humanness to help others be the best that they could be, grow closer to God, and be loving to others.

THE ASSIGNMENT

Too many people never connect with their purpose and mission on this planet. Answer the questions below thinking about what significant impact you want to make in this world. These goals can be partially met through your career, but should not be limited to what you can accomplish in your career.

Thinking about myself as a whole person:

I believe that I have been blessed with the following three gifts or abilities…

_____

_____

_____

I have the greatest passion in life when I am…

_____

_____

_____

I feel closest to my purpose when I…

_____

_____

_____

Now the big question:

How will you channel the above to create a life of significance?

_____

_____

_____

ELIMINATING INTEGRITY CHALLENGES

*If a house is divided against itself,
that house cannot stand.*

—Christian Bible, New International Version, Mark 3:25

THE RESEARCH: When We Don't Practice What We Preach

Cognitive dissonance is a well-studied psychological principle that helps us understand how we handle inconsistencies between different internal beliefs and between beliefs and behavior.

The classic experiment involved a group of subjects who were involved in doing an extremely mundane and boring task. After they were done with the task these individuals were asked to tell the next group of subjects that the task was exciting and fun. In other words, they were asked to lie. One group was told that if they would tell the next group how great the experiment was then they would be given twenty dollars. The other group was given the same instructions, but was only offered one dollar for their efforts. After each of the groups misrepresented the experiment the experimenters asked them how interesting they truly found the experiment. Who do you think found the experiment genuinely more interesting? Do you think it was the group that received twenty dollars or the group that received one dollar?

When I use this example in workshops on confidence, most people guess that the twenty-dollar group found the experiment more interesting. In this case, most people are wrong. The research showed that the individuals who were paid one dollar said that they genuinely found the experiment more interesting. To explain this we have to go back to the dilemma. These people were asked, in essence, to lie about their level of interest in the experiment. However, most people believe that lying is wrong. Therefore there was a gap between what they believed and what they did. This gap creates dissonance or tension that feels uncomfortable to us. Since most people don't like discomfort there is a motivation to rid ourselves of this mental tension. The group that received twenty dollars were able to decrease the tension by justifying their willingness to lie because they got paid twenty dollars for it (sad, but true—$20.00 was enough justification). The group that received one dollar could not justify it. "I'm willing to lie for one dollar" isn't something that most people want to believe about themselves. Therefore, the only way to rid themselves of the dissonance or tension was to start truly believing that the experiment was not that boring. Once they convinced themselves that the experiment wasn't that bad, the dissonance decreased. They convinced themselves that since the experiment was interesting, they hadn't really lied.

Reference: Festinger, 1957.

THE APPLICATION

The word "integrity" has multiple meanings, but one meaning when referring to our psyche is the idea of being fully integrated or consistent. The extreme example for lack of integration is the individual with multiple personality disorder. A more common lack of integrity is when we have competing beliefs or when our behavior does not match our beliefs. While common, the lack of integration can be a huge threat to full confidence.

When our beliefs are in conflict, one has to eventually give. When our behavior does not match what we believe then we will live in tension and a state of limbo until something changes. This is why (and I speak from personal experience) people who are out of integrity will often sabotage their success. Deep down they don't feel they deserve to be successful because they are in a state of internal warfare (even when they block it out consciously).

Just imagine any other situation in which you would have some tension or competing issues. Imagine a track team where some members of the team ran one way while the others ran the opposite way. Sometimes they would smash into each other, but they certainly would not reach the goal. Compare that with runners all sprinting in the same direction. They will reach the goal without team conflict or opposing performance. Of course, they would win the race against the conflicting team every time!

Integrity gets down to these questions: Who are you? When everything else is stripped away what kind of person are you? What do you really believe? How consistent are you in living your personal values in your work or have you sacrificed that for a paycheck? Does the way you treat others reflect your spiritual beliefs? Confident people seem to know who they are. They are integrated in belief and action and are consistent in word and in action. As long as you feel guilt, shame, or even confusion about who you are or what you do, you will have a barrier between yourself and maximum confidence.

THE ASSIGNMENT

Revealing your own cognitive dissonance can be a painful exercise. We will do all sorts of things from drinking heavily to keeping too busy to staying angry with others to hide our own dissonance from ourselves. One way to truly reveal any dissonance is to ask someone whom you trust this question: "Where do you see my behavior not matching what I say or believe?" Yes, it is a really tough question to ask and you have to be ready to get an answer. To try to discover areas of dissonance on your own, try the following chart. In the first column I have listed several common values. Record your belief concerning that value. For example, under "what is success?" you might put "providing well for my family" or you could put "being in the top 1% income bracket in this country" or you might put "serving God." Put your true belief or beliefs in that box. Then, in the next column, record examples of your behavior matching your beliefs. In the next column be honest with occasions where your behavior did not match your beliefs. In the final column, record any commitments you are willing to make to decrease your dissonance. To my knowledge your two main ways to do this are either to change your behavior to match your belief or change your belief to match your behavior. You decide.

Don't worry if this chart reveals some dissonance for you. In fact, worry more if it does not reveal any dissonance. If it doesn't, you may not be being honest with yourself. However, if dissonance is revealed, it just means you're human, so strive toward decreasing this dissonance and living a life free of being at war with yourself. You will notice the impact on your confidence almost immediately.

Cognitive Dissonance Chart

Question	Your belief	Matching behaviors	Contradictory behaviors	My commitment
How do you define success?				
What are the top 3 character traits people should have?				
What spiritual guidelines should people live by?				
What habits would you like to change? Why?				

GRACE: CONNECTING TO GOD

Dear God, Please protect us from splinters and owies and help us not to walk on the table and mess up our food.

—My son Vance Ursiny at age 3 (praying over our dinner)

THE RESEARCH: Where is Your Focus?

Are you preoccupied more with what you don't have or do you live in gratitude for what you have been blessed with? Abraham Maslow spent much of his focus on the tendency toward growth and development. He named two tendencies worth mentioning here:

Deficiency orientation: preoccupation with things we do not have (usually material items)

Growth orientation: focusing on what is available in life (usually about what we have and can do)

When we are focused on growth orientation then we can have what Maslow called "peak experiences" in which we fully get to experience being alive and grow to our potential.

Reference: Maslow, 1971.

THE APPLICATION

Jeff wanted to party and see the world and could not wait until the proper time to receive the inheritance from his father. His father was a well to do business owner who had done some decent estate planning and had saved quite a bit of money that his son would receive upon his death. Jeff's philosophy was, "Why should I have to wait for my father to die to get what is going to be mine anyway?" So, given his arrogant nature he actually went to his father and boldly asked to get his money in advance. He wanted it now, so that he could get out and see the world. His father loved him very much and instead of taking a tough love approach to Jeff, actually ended up giving him every cent of his inheritance. He kept only the inheritance that was going to go to Jeff's brother Dave (who seemed to have the patience to wait until the proper time to get his money). So Jeff's father gave Jeff the money and watched his son leave without a thank you to go "see the world." And see the world he did. Jeff loved a good time and he loved for others to have a good time with him. He traveled the world and blew thousands upon thousands of dollars on every kind of pleasure you could think of. He partied, he paid for friends to party, he spent money left and right and lived like a prince for a short time. He paid for sex, he paid for gourmet food, he bought the finest wines, he experimented with all types of drugs, he basically paid for anything that was fun. But as life tends to go, the money eventually ran out. Suddenly, all of his partying friends seemed far less interested in hanging out with him. In fact, they pretty much ignored him once he could no longer pay for their fun. Penniless, muddled by long-term drug use and ignored by his so-called former friends, he began to live on the streets. He tried getting odd jobs, most of which barely paid minimum wage, but his physical smell and deteriorated looks made him an unappealing job candidate. He was poor, burned out, and a mental mess. At times he would even eat from garbage cans just to get some food in his stomach (not quite the fine dining from the past). Finally, he swallowed his pride and decided to return to his father and ask his dad if he could work at some menial job in his father's company.

Jeff was approaching his father's office when his dad spotted him in the parking lot. Jeff's father went flying out of his office, ran down the stairs and outside to grab Jeff with the biggest bear hug you can imagine. He didn't care that his son was dirty and smelly; he was just overjoyed that his son had returned to him. His father brought Jeff into the office and announced to everyone that he was going to throw a huge party to honor Jeff's return and he wanted to give Jeff a position of prominence in the company (you can imagine all of the office workers' reactions to this).

Jeff's brother, Dave, was watching all of this with amazement (he was now a VP in the company). As his father continued to gush over Jeff, Dave became more and more angry. His father had not thrown a big party for him! He felt he had earned his position in the company, and Jeff was going to get a great position just for showing up? It felt incredibly unfair. So as his anger continued to grow, Dave went to talk to his father. "How could you do this? I have been loyal to you all of my life and you have never treated me this well! This is unfair and wrong!" accused Dave. His father looked at him with grace and tenderness in his eyes and said, "I love you and appreciate your loyalty over these years very, very much. However, your brother has returned to us and it is now time to celebrate his return. He was lost to us and now he is back. Come celebrate."

In the Christian Bible there is a story called "The Prodigal Son." It is a parable told by Christ about a young man who went to his father and asked for his inheritance early and misspent it. It is also the story of his brother who felt it was unfair that his brother, who failed so terribly, would be welcomed with such open arms. My story of Jeff is my attempt at telling the same parable in today's cultural terms. I think the message stays consistent. God gives grace to those who fall. God celebrates when someone has completely screwed up their life and comes back to Him. And we should too.

Instead, we often feel like we have to earn our grace. I've had clients say, "He doesn't deserve to be forgiven." When I hear this, I look directly into their eyes and tell them that they are absolutely right—the person who hurt them doesn't "deserve" it. In fact you can't really forgive someone who deserves it. If they deserve it, then there really isn't something to forgive. Forgiveness is about grace, not what is fair.

For what do you need grace in your life? In what ways do you desire grace from yourself, grace from others, and grace from God? The truly confident person must embrace the fact that we are flawed. When I was younger I had never "gotten" the prodigal son story. In fact, I always identified more with the brother who had always been loyal. It was until my later years that I was convicted of the fact that I was the younger brother. I had fallen so far from who I thought I was and wanted to be. However, the humility and conviction that has come from facing that fact that I am just as flawed as everyone else on this planet and will never be immune to mistakes (even big ones) has given me a peace and a humility that I did not have before. In short, it has increased my true confidence.

My prayer every day is that I am forgiven for my shortcomings, that I may not cause harm to another human being, that I prosper greatly and that my life fall within the will of God. What is your prayer?

THE ASSIGNMENT

Develop a prayer that shows the desires of your heart. Write down a prayer that embraces your humanity and at the same time encourages you to be more. The prayer should be your own and from the depths of your heart. However, if you need some help getting started I have a couple of examples that I use. If you are distracted by the fact that my examples are Christian in nature, then I simply encourage you to accept that these examples represent what I believe is true. However, as long as I openly share my faith, I feel no responsibility to convince you of what you need to believe. That is between you and God. I trust that if we all keep an open mind and earnestly pray that truth is revealed to us then we are going to be blessed with truth. I constantly pray for truth. I know I don't have all of the answers. I just want to be willing to hear them (even if I don't like them).

It is only when we shut down possibilities or insist that we know the complete truth or hate others of different viewpoints, that I believe we disappoint God greatly. If you ask God to reveal Himself to you, and are willing to truly accept what he reveals, then whatever happens is likely what should happen. So I share these examples as consistent with my beliefs. You can do with them what you will.

Prayer #1: A general approach

Thank you for _____

_____

Please help me _____

_____

Please bless me with _____

_____

Bless others, specifically _____
with _____

Help me live my life in such a way that _____

_____

In all of this help me to serve you well and always honor those gifts that you have given me. Help me to submit to what you want for my life, not just what I want. Please reveal the truth to me and help me realize who you truly are and what you want me to be and do. Amen

Prayer #2: From the Christian Bible, but made popular in *The Prayer of Jabez: Breaking Through to the Blessed Life* by Bruce Wilkinson:
Oh, that you would bless me indeed, and enlarge my territory, that your hand would be with me, and that you would keep me from evil, that I may not cause pain.

Prayer #3: Christ's prayer (From the book of Matthew in the Christian Bible)
Our Father in heaven, hallowed be your name, your kingdom come, your will be done on earth as it is in heaven. Give us today our daily bread. Forgive us our debts, as we also have forgiven our debtors. And lead us not into temptation, but deliver us from the evil one.

Prayer #4: Other
If none of these formats work for you, write your own prayer here. Make it deep and from your heart:

_____

_____

_____

BUILDING A PERSONAL MISSION STATEMENT

Our deepest fear is not that we are inadequate. Our deepest fear is that we are powerful beyond measure. It is our light, not our darkness that most frightens us. We ask ourselves, who am I to be brilliant, gorgeous, talented, fabulous? Actually, who are you not to be? You are a child of God. Your playing small does not serve the world. There is nothing enlightened about shrinking so that other people won't feel insecure around you.

—Marianne Williamson

THE RESEARCH: Your Future Self

What is your vision of yourself in the future? As you imagine the future, are you more or less successful in fulfilling your mission and purpose? Research indicates that thinking about yourself as successful creates greater persistence on difficult tasks as compared to people who think about themselves as failing. Building a personal mission statement and having a vision of success can help you make the impact that you want to make in this world with confidence and effectiveness.

Reference: Ruvolo & Markus, 1992.

THE APPLICATION

Jan never planned on being a multimillionaire; she just hated bullies. Her dislike for bullies was only second to her love and care for those in unfortunate circumstances. In fact, as a young woman in her twenties Jan would invite prostitutes over for meals and try to talk to them about breaking free of their lives. In her thirties, despite having only a high school education, she was a highly successful salesperson. However, her prospects were limited due to her lack of formal education. Eventually she decided to start her own company, but she wanted a company that would allow anyone to achieve the level of success that he or she wanted despite background, race, education, or other factors.

Her company is Personal Preference, Inc., and they sell art by giving private consultations, fundraisers, and group presentations. Through an extensive training program she has created an opportunity that allows anyone who is willing to work hard to make a significant income and to impact the lives of others. God has blessed her richly and I have had the pleasure of consulting for her company for many years now. No other company of this size that I know of spends as much money and time as Jan does on helping her people improve and grow.

Jan had a mission (she still does) and that mission was not about getting rich; it was about impacting lives and creating a fair playing ground for people. It was about growing people and helping them become what they wanted to be despite any obstacles. Jan didn't set out to be a millionaire, but she is and she gives far more back to this world than she has ever taken. If you can't tell, I have a great deal of respect for her and consider it a privilege to be a small part of her mission.

What is your mission? What tugs at your heartstrings? I don't care about your income bracket or your title or your abilities, you can give back to this world. You can either take from it or give to it. What I have found is that the people that tend to give the most, especially in helping others, are at greater peace with themselves, are more satisfied with their success, and are more confident than those who sit back and complain about what life hasn't given them.

What is your mission? It doesn't have to be huge (but then again, it doesn't have to be small). It just has to be yours. Confidence is solidified in purpose. Living your mission is an antidote to insecurity.

THE ASSIGNMENT

The first coach that I worked with was helpful in giving me a formula for developing my personal mission statement. For me, I needed something simple and to the point. Here is the mission statement formula that he suggested. Use the following formula to write out your own mission statement:

The purpose of my life and work is to (list the objectives; what you want to accomplish)

_____

_____

_____

This relates to my identity of (list your core characteristics or values):

_____

_____

_____

I will do this for (list who will be the recipients of your life purpose):

_____

_____

_____

I will accomplish this by (list the behaviors or activities that you will use to live out your purpose):

_____

_____

_____

The value that this will bring to the world is (list the benefits to others and the world):

_____

_____

_____

APPLYING YOUR SPIRITUAL STRATEGIES

Case Study

"I don't need God," he said. "I've lived a pretty good life, I'm happy, and I make a ton of money; what more could I want?" Peter was serious. He felt like life was great and God was invented for the weak and the unsuccessful.

"I don't deserve to be forgiven for the things I have done in my life," came out of Peter's mouth a year later. Peter had been in conflict with his boss, was likely losing his job, had a wife who said she didn't even know who he was anymore, and was flooded with thoughts of past failures. This man who arrogantly proclaimed to me that he didn't need God was now crying out for help. It was a horrible time for Peter and absolutely the best thing that ever happened to him in his life.

Proverbs 16:18 states "Pride goes before destruction and a haughty spirit before a fall." I cannot tell you how many times this has proven to be true, both in my own life and in the lives of my clients. It scares me when people are too judgmental of others (been there, done that), it frightens me when people claim, "Oh, I could never do that," and I tremble when I hear someone say that he doesn't need God because I know what is likely coming. Peter was experiencing several consequences of his arrogance and pride.

There were several underlying issues made clear during my work with Peter. First, he and his boss were in conflict because Peter's job had transformed over the year to something that did not excite him or play to his gifts properly. Neither of them fully realized that the job mismatch was the main source of conflict. Peter was walking into the office with tension (dissonance) each day and was angry about the workplace changes and unfulfilling tasks. He had lost all sense of a greater purpose to his life.

Peter was also forty-four, so it was a natural time of reexamination, reviewing his successes, and wondering about the impact that he would leave on his family, friends, and community. As he reassessed it, despite his great financial success, it just wasn't enough. His coaching was a five-month journey into discovering his passions, talents and mission. We probed into causes of his mental tension and found conflicting beliefs about God, past actions, and self-image. Our work helped Peter integrate these different thoughts to find beliefs and actions that were more consistent with each other.

In the end, Peter left his job. It had transformed to something that no longer fit who he wanted to be and what he wanted to do.

He took a huge risk as well as a hefty pay cut to pursue a passion career. To be honest, this change is recent, and as of the time of this writing neither Peter nor I know how the journey will end. He still goes back and forth on God's role in his life, but knows that he needs God and is on a path to try and figure out what that looks like and means for him. He is trusting God and asking for guidance with his choices. He is a far more humble man and in my eyes, a far better human being. I believe that his choices will be honored and that he will have an awesome impact on those around him. He is connected with his spiritual self and is trying hard to let that lead him where he needs to go. That is basically all that any of us can do—isn't it?

The Challenge

Review the spiritual strategies presented in the five previous chapters. Which seem most helpful to you?

- Using the Career Projection Exercise as a template to pursue your vocational calling
- Focusing on your purpose and gifts to live confidently
- Breaking free of integrity challenges and dissonance that threaten your success and your confidence
- Using a daily prayer to build your spiritual confidence
- Developing and practicing your mission statement

Take at least one of these techniques and make a commitment to how you will apply it on a regular basis in your life. Write your commitment to yourself here:

I commit to _____

_____

_____

I will do this every _____

_____

_____

CONCLUSION:

WHAT TO DO IN THE NEXT 6 WEEKS

If you have stuck it all the way to this point then I congratulate and thank you. I congratulate you because it took persistence and focus to do this and I am sure that you have grown as a result of your efforts. I thank you because it is truly a privilege that you allowed me to walk with you via this book on this part of your journey. Will you be successful in truly using this book to continue to impact your confidence to the next level? I hope and believe so. Make sure you keep the habits that you committed to previously at the end of each section and set a date in six weeks to review your progress. If in six weeks you haven't seen the improvement that you would like to have seen I encourage you to go back through the book again. You can grow with multiple readings of this book and remember to never stop.

I love hearing success stories and if you feel like this book has aided you please drop me an email at Drtim@advantagecoaching.com.

While I can't promise to reply to every email, I will promise to read them and to celebrate with you your next level of confidence.

Blessings to you as we all continue to grow.

ADDITIONAL EXERCISES

These are additional questions and exercises for many of the sections in this book. Complete those related to chapters which spoke most closely to your confidence challenges.

1.3

Complete the following additional questions concerning your internal thermostat:

Away from goal (this is the level of success that you will not allow yourself to go below)

•　Most of us make a subconscious vow as children concerning something we will never allow ourselves to do or be. Some common examples are "I will never go hungry," "I will never be like my mother," and "I will never be picked on again." Think of the most impactful time in your youth. If you can make it conscious, write your conscious or subconscious vow(s) here:

I will never: _____

_____

Toward goal (this is the level of success that you are moving to right now)

- All of us are working toward something today (even if it is simply a paycheck). What is the main goal that you are working toward presently that you feel confident that you will achieve?

I know that I will:

1.4
Answer these additional questions about your greatest challenge:

1. One way that I have developed positively from this experience as a person is...

   _____

   _____

2. If I choose to see it in a strength-building light, then I am grateful that I went through this difficulty because...

   _____

   _____

1.5

Answer the following additional questions related to the automobile analogy:

Rearview mirror

1. How did your relationship with your parents and siblings impact your confidence?

   _____

   _____

2. How did peer relationships impact your confidence growing up?

   _____

   _____

Side view mirror

1. What is the main habit that you have currently that could hold you back from your maximum success in life?

   _____

   _____

2. What is your commitment about this habit?

   _____

   _____

Blind spot

Ask a loved one, good friend, mentor or anyone that you fully trust the following more detailed questions:

1. What natural talents or gifts do you think I have? (I know it sounds arrogant, but tell them I made you ask.)

    _____

    _____

2. What do you think are my biggest strengths that I'm not maximizing to their peak potential?

    _____

    _____

3. What do you think is the biggest weakness I have that I don't see about myself?

    _____

    _____

2.4

Let's make some more positive predictions for your future using a ten-year time frame:

Within ten years:

I am going to accomplish _____

_____

I will definitely _____

_____

I will impact _____ by doing

_____

My greatest hope is that I will _____

_____

2.6

Create these additional affirmations:

1. Something that I can do now that I could not do five years ago is:

   _____

   _____

2. My greatest work achievement is:

   _____

   _____

3. I want to be confident enough to:

   _____

   _____

3.2

Keep your journal next to your bed and when you wake up immediately grab the journal and start writing. Record the dreams that you had that night in as much detail as possible. Our dreams are often windows into the deepest of our wants and fears. What does your dream suggest about your inner desires or concerns? For example, if you have a dream about using a steamroller to roll over this book, then picking it up, tearing it in two, and throwing it in a fire, then your inner life might be suggesting that you have some resistance to growing your confidence!

3.3

Look at the ten words you created to describe yourself at your best. Then answer the following questions:

1. Come up with one example from the past month where you fully showed most of these attributes:

   _____

   _____

2. Describe one example from this month when you did not fully show these gifts that you have. What can you learn about this event? Is there anyone that you need to talk to in order to take 100% accountability for your behavior? If so, when will you do it?

   _____

   _____

3.5

Let's get even more specific with your music, art, and movie choices.

What music, art, and movies get you out of a bad mood?

Music:

_____

_____

_____

Art:

_____

_____

_____

Movies:

_____

_____

_____

What music, art, and movies center you?

Music:

_____

_____

_____

Art:

_____

_____

_____

Movies:

_____

_____

_____

What music, art, and movies connect you with your feelings?

Music:

_____

_____

_____

Art:

_____

_____

_____

Movies:

_____

_____

_____

4.2

Take your top drainer in each of the following categories and build an action plan to address it.

Things I can't impact or control

You only have two good choices with something you can't impact whatsoever. You can either embrace it or avoid it (it makes no sense to fight it, since it is just like beating your head against a brick wall). Make a decision about which action you would like to do with your choice. To embrace it means that you fully accept that it exists and will not change, but that you will no longer drain yourself by being upset about it or trying to change it. To avoid it means that you also refuse to allow it to drain you, but that you accomplish this by getting that activity or person out of your life. For example, if the nightly news drains you, the choices are to either quit watching it or watch it and embrace that we live in a complicated world (but quit being shocked by the bad news). So what is your choice? Write your answer here:

_____

_____

_____

Things I can impact, but can't control

With your top drainer that you can't control, but may be able to impact, what impact would you like to have? For example, if you are working with a critical person you likely can't control his nature. However, you may have some activities that you could try to set boundaries around how you will allow him to talk with you. So what will you do (what actions will you take) to impact the item that you chose in this category? Write your answer here:

_____

_____

_____

4.5

Again think about a great performance from the past and answer these additional questions:

How did you feel physically? Where physically did you feel it?

_____

_____

What was it about your attitude that got you there?

_____

_____

What are other reasons that you performed so well?

_____

_____

5.2

Add these questions to your assessment of your community. Answer the following questions to help make a decision concerning potential drainers in your life:

1. Why do you allow people to drain you? What is your part in creating this dynamic?

   _____

   _____

2. What approaches have you tried in order to change the way drainers interact with you? What has had impact and what does not work?

   _____

   _____

6.3

Finish these additional thoughts to help identify your purpose:

1. I have the greatest peace in life when I...

   _____

   _____

2. I get the most compliments in life when I...

   _____

   _____

6.4

Fill in these additional areas in your cognitive dissonance chart:

Cognitive Dissonance Chart

Question	Your belief	Matching behaviors	Contradictory behaviors	My commitment
What do you want to accomplish vocationally?				
How should people treat each other?				
What do you believe about life balance?				
What other beliefs are important to you?				

BIBLIOGRAPHY

Anderson, A. K., & Phelps, E. A. 2000. Expression without recognition: Contributions of the human amygdala to emotional communication. Psychological Science 11:106–111.

Ashcraft, M. H. 2002. *Cognition* (3rd ed.). Upper Saddle River, NJ: Prentice-Hall.

Bandler, R. & Grinder, J. 1975. *The structure of magic: a book about language and therapy: Volume I.* Alto, CA: Science & Behavior Books.

Bandura, A. 2001. Social cognitive theory: An agentic approach. *Annual Review of Psychology* 52:1–26.

Bandura, A. & Cervone, D. 1983. Self-evaluative and self-efficacy mechanisms governing the motivational effects of gal systems. *Journal of Personality and Social Psychology* 45:1017–1028.

Bernstein, Douglas A., Penner, Louis A., Clarke-Stewart, Alison. Roy, Edward J. 2003. *Psychology*. Boston, MA: Houghton Mifflin.

Buckingham, M. & Clifton, D. 2001. *Now discover your strengths*. New York: The Free Press.

Cohen, S., & Herbert, T.B. 1996. Health Psychology: Psychology factors and physical disease from the human perspective of human psychoneuroimmunology. *Annual review of psychology* 47:113–142.

Ellis, A. 1995. Rational emotive behavior therapy. In R. J. Corsini & D. Wedding, eds., *Current psychotherapies* (5th ed). Itasca, IL. Peacock.

Erikson, E. H. 1968. *Identity: Youth and crisis.* New York: Norton.

Evans, J. St. B. T., Handley, S. J., Harper, C. N. J., & Johnson-Laird, P.N. 1999. Reasoning about necessity and possibility: A test of the mental model theory of deduction. *Journal of Experimental Psychology: Learning, Memory, and Cognition* 25:1495–1513.

Faulkner, C. *NLP: The Technology of Achievement.* Chicago: Nightingale Conant.

Festinger, L. 1957. *A theory of cognitive dissonance.* Evanston, IL: Row, Petersen.

Gilbert, D.T., & Malone, P. S. 1995. The correspondence bias. *Psychological Bulletin* 117:21–38.

Goleman, D. 1997. *Emotional Intelligence: Why It Can Matter More Than IQ.* New York: Bantam Books.

Goleman, D., Boyatzis, R., McKee, A. 2002. *Primal Leadership: Realizing the Power of Emotional Intelligence.* Boston, MA: Harvard Business School Press.

Hull, C.L. 1943. *Principles of behavior.* New York: Appleton-Century-Crofts.

James, W. 1890. *Principles of psychology.* New York: Holt.

Janowiak, J.J., & Hackman, R. 1994. Meditation and college students' self-actualization and rated stress. *Psychological Reports* 752:1007–1010.

Kanter, Rosabeth Moss. 2004. Confidence: *How winning streaks and losing streaks begin and end.* New York: Crown Business.

Kenrick, D. T., Neuberg, S.L., & Cialdini, R.B. 2002. *Social psychology: Unraveling the mystery* (2nd ed.). Boston: Allyn and Bacon.

Lazarus, R. S. 1991. *Emotion and adaptation.* New York: Oxford University Press.

Markus, H. R., Kitayama, S. 1991. Culture and the self: Implications for cognition, emotion, and motivation. *Psychology Review* 98:224–253.

Maslow, A.H. 1971. *The farther reaches of human nature.* New York: McGraw-Hill.

Öst, L. G., Svensson, L., Hellström, K., & Lindwall, R. 2001. One-session treatment of specific phobias in youths: A randomized clinical trial. *Journal of Consulting and Clinical Psychology* 69:814–824.

Maston, A. & Coatsworth, J. 1998. The development of competence in favorable and unfavorable environments: Lessons from research on successful children. *American Psychologist* 5:205–220.

McGinnis, A. L. 1987. *Confidence: how to succeed at being yourself.* Minneapolis: Augsburg Publishing House.

Niven, D. 2002. *The 100 simple secrets of successful people: What scientists have learned and how you can use it.* New York: HarperCollins.

Oysermann, S. 2001. Self-concept and identity. In A. Tesser & N. Schwarz (eds.), *Blackwell handbook of social psychology: Intraindividual processes* (499–517). Oxford, England: Blackwell.

Ost, L. G. 1989. One-session treatment for specific phobias. *Behavioral Research and Therapy* 27:1–7. In Gray, P. 1994. *Psychology* (2nd. ed.). New York: Worth.

Pajares, F., & Schunk, D.H., 2001. Self-beliefs and school success: Self-efficacy, self concept and school achievement. In R. Riding and S. Rayner (eds.), *Self-perception* (239–266). London: Ablex Publishing.

Pettigrew, T. F., & Tropp, L. R. 2000. Does intergroup contact reduce prejudice? Recent meta-analytic findings. In S. Oskamp (ed.), *Reducing prejudice and discrimination* (93–114). Mahwah, NJ: Erlbaum.

Phelan, Thomas. 1995. 1-2-3 Magic: *Effective discipline for children 2–12*. Child Management.

Piper, Watty, Hauman, George, & Hauman, Doris. 1978. *The little engine that could*. New York. Platt & Munk.

Robeson, R. 1998. College students on the rebound. PhD dissertation, Indiana University.

Rogers, C. R. 1961. *On becoming a person*. Boston: Houghton Mifflin.

Rosen, R. 1991. *The healthy company*. Los Angeles: Tarcher.

Ruvolo, A. P., & Markus, H. R. 1992. Possible selves and performance: The power of self-relevant imagery. *Social Cognition* 10:95–124.

Sakairi, Y. 1992. Studies on meditation using questionnaires. *Japanese Psychological Review* 351:94–112.

Schwarz, N., & Bohner, G. 2001. The construction of attitudes. In A. Tesser & N. Schwarz (eds.), *Blackwell handbook of social psychology: Intraindividual processes* (436–457).

Seligman, M. E. P. 1975. *Helplessness: On depression, development, and death*. San Francisco: Freeman.

Seligman, M. 1998. *Learned Optimism: How to Change Your Mind and Your Life*. New York. Pocket Books.

Spencer, S., Steele, C.M., & Quinn, D. 1997. *Under suspicion on inability: Stereotype threats and women's math performance*. Unpublished manuscript.

Troop, L. R., & Wright, S. 2001. In group identification as the inclusion of in group in the self. *Personality and Social Psychology Bulletin* 27:585–600.

Ursiny, Timothy E., 2003. *The coward's guide to conflict: Empowering solutions for those who would rather run than fight*. Naperville, IL: Sourcebooks, Inc.

Wilkinson, Bruce H. 2000. *The prayer of Jabez*. Sisters, OR: Multnomah Publishers, Inc.

Wilson, A. E., & Ross, M. 2000. The frequency of temporal-self and social comparisons in people's personal appraisals. *Journal of Personality and Social Psychology* 78:928–942.

Wolpe, J. 1958. *Psychotherapy by reciprocal inhibition*. Stanford, CA: Stanford University Press.

Wolpe, J. 1973. *The practice of behavior therapy* (2nd ed.). Oxford: Pergamon.

LINKS TO FREE RESOURCES (FOR TRAINERS, COACHES, AND INDIVIDUALS)

I am dedicated to helping others grow in confidence and I have a team in my company, Advantage Coaching & Training, that shares this mission with me and are willing to give of their time and energy to help others. If you have bought a copy of this book then you are entitled to some complimentary resources on our website, www.advantagecoaching.com. Since this book is intended for both individual and professional use, we have provided resources for each group.

For Individuals

We offer free introductory confidence group teleclasses to help individuals walk through exercises in this book and build their confidence to the next level. These classes are conducted over the phone in groups via a conference line. The only cost to you is your regular cost of a long distance call. You can find a link to the schedule of classes on our home page.

If desired, you can also arrange for a short complimentary coaching session for one of our coaches to help you use this book in the most effective manner or address any topic related to self-improvement and growth (subject to demand).

For Trainers and Team Leaders

We want you to use this book to train others to their next level of confidence. Therefore, you can find training outlines on our website that you may use at no charge as long as participants each purchase a copy of this book. On the website you will find guides for half day and full day trainings as well as suggested training guides for team leaders to incorporate confidence building in their regular team meetings.

For Coaches

Few interventions can be more effective for building up someone's confidence than working one-on-one with a coach. Therefore, we occasionally provide complimentary "coach the coaches" programs in a teleclass format.

For Corporations

We give keynote addresses, trainings, brown bag lunches, team facilitation and one-on-one coaching around confidence building for your teams and key employees. We offer initial telephone consultations at no charge. To get a full description for how to build a culture of confidence in the workplace, follow the link on our home page.

For All Groups

We have provided additional quotes, more movie, art, and music ideas, as well as other material related to the book. These are complimentary to anyone who purchases *The Confidence Plan*.

To access these benefits simply go to www.advantagecoaching.com and follow the links on the home page. We look forward to aiding you to impact your confidence and the confidence of those around you!

ABOUT THE AUTHOR

Tim Ursiny, PhD, CBC, RCC, is the president and founder of Advantage Coaching & Training. He is a success coach and trainer specializing in helping people reach peak performance and happiness. He is dedicated toward helping people see their strengths and create the lives they want. His primary areas of focus are confidence, communication and coaching skills.

Dr. Ursiny (usually referred to as "Dr. Tim") received his undergraduate degree from Wheaton College and his doctorate in psychology from Northern Illinois University. He is a member of the Worldwide Association of Business Coaches, the International Coach Federation, and the Chicagoland Chapter of the American Society for Training and Development.

He regularly speaks for Fortune 500 companies wanting workshops that are practical, yet entertaining. He also regularly coaches CEOs, executives, and others on a variety of subjects related to performance and life satisfaction.

Dr. Tim's previous work, *The Coward's Guide to Conflict*, is in its third printing at the time of this writing and has been translated into several foreign languages.

He lives in Wheaton, Illinois with his wife, Marla, and his three sons, Zach, Colton, and Vance.

Dr. Tim can be reached at Drtim@advantagecoaching.com.

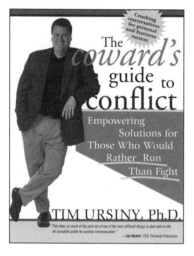

The Coward's Guide to Conflict is available at online booksellers and at a bookstore near you.